Editor:
Jodi L. McClay, M.A.

Project Manager:
Paul Gardner

Editor in Chief:
Sharon Coan, M.S. Ed.

Art Director:
Elayne Roberts

Art Coordination Assistant:
Cheri Macoubrie Wilson

Cover Artist:
Tina DeLeon Macabitas

Product Manager:
Phil Garcia

Imaging:
Ralph Olmedo Jr.

Publishers:
Rachelle Cracchiolo, M.S. Ed.
Mary Dupuy Smith, M.S. Ed.

W9-CDL-292

INTEGRATING TECHNOLOGY
into the
Social Studies Curriculum

INTERMEDIATE

Authors:

Bruce Michael Green and William Oksner

Teacher Created Materials, Inc.
6421 Industry Way
Westminster, CA 92683
www.teachercreated.com

ISBN-1-57690-431-8

©1999 Teacher Created Materials, Inc.
Reprinted, 1999
Made in U.S.A.

TABLE OF CONTENTS

INTRODUCTION

Now more than ever technology is impacting all aspects of society and societal development. That is why it is imperative that students not only learn how to use technology but also understand the impact and influence—both positive and negative—of technology on the direction of human development. The social studies curriculum provides an excellent opportunity to do both, and *Integrating Technology into the Curriculum (Intermediate)* is designed with that in mind.

In the lesson plans that follow, you and your class will explore many different aspects of social studies, using various technologies and media. The activities are divided into 10 thematic categories based on the National Council for the Social Studies standards. This thematic approach provides a framework easily customized to fit your specific social studies needs.

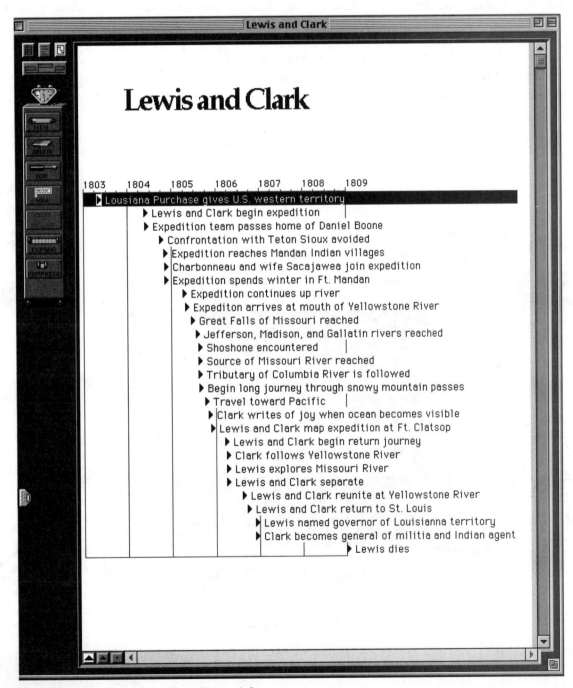

From Tom Snyder Production's *TimeLiner* 4.0

WHY SOCIAL STUDIES?

Social studies, one could argue, is the metadiscipline. After all, it is the study of what we as human beings do—past, present, and future—and therefore every other discipline falls under its auspices. The advantage of this perspective is that it makes linking social studies to other subject areas easy. The challenge is developing a cohesive social studies curriculum that encompasses the broad scope of the subject.

Because curricula vary from state to state and school to school, the lesson plans in *Integrating Technology into the Social Studies Curriculum (Intermediate)* focus on a process that results in specific content. Each lesson is complete and ready to use but it should be seen as more of a template for teaching a social studies concept, one into which you can then place specific information from your particular curriculum. The open-ended nature of the lesson plans also makes them ideal for developing an interdisciplinary curriculum and exploring a math/science/social studies link.

The activities in this book are designed to be flexible enough to allow plenty of opportunity to incorporate your favorite textbook, articles, and activities. While we frequently suggest that students work in groups (social studies in action!), the lessons will work fine when performed individually.

WHY TECHNOLOGY?

Often in education we are pressured to integrate new technologies into our classrooms just because they are new. We are forced to restructure the way we do things in order to incorporate the latest and greatest gadget. Frequently, this gadget finds itself by the educational wayside rather quickly. Radio, filmstrip, and television are three "revolutionary educational technologies" that have not lived up to their glittering promise.

Therefore, it is important to remember to start with and focus on our classroom and curricular goals when thinking about technology or any educational buzzword. We must decide what meaningful content we want to cover, what interactions we want to have in our classrooms, and what skills our students must attain—basically, what our end goals are—prior to attempting to integrate technology.

Skills and goals, such as becoming great readers, fluent writers, critical thinkers, and responsible citizens, tend to be universal and lasting, unlike "revolutionary technologies." Once we set our classroom skill and content goals, we can then ask what tools are available to help us achieve the goals. When we use technology to help us achieve meaningful goals, it will not follow the path of the filmstrip, radio, and television. When we use technology for the sake of the technology, it will quickly end up as a coat room doorstop.

Three helpful questions to ask when thinking about using technology are the following:

- Does it help you do what you love to do?
- Does it help you do what you hate to do?
- Does it help you do something you couldn't do before?

Helping You Do What You Love to Do

Do you love classroom discussions and thrive on the interaction, tension, and drama of role-playing simulations? Do you love small group activities and the collaborative learning they promote? Do you love classroom newspapers or other projects? If the answers to these questions is yes, you probably realize how time-intensive and draining all these activities can be. Technology can help! A computer can aid in the planning, implementation, and follow-through of these kinds of meaningful activities.

Helping You Do What You Hate to Do

Often, using technology just to take care of "administrivia," such as writing letters to parents, grading, and creating tests and work sheets—the things we didn't get into teaching to do—can be beneficial to both you and your students. Even if your students don't have direct use of the technologies, teacher-tool software will help you with necessary tasks and free-up your time, giving you more time to do what you do best, have a positive, learning relationship with your students.

Helping You Do What You Couldn't Do Before

Some technologies allow us to do things we couldn't have done before, or couldn't have done very easily. For example, a database program allows the user to quickly and easily manipulate large amounts of information, run correlations and comparative analyses, and print high quality graphs, charts, and posters at the touch of a button; a desktop publisher allows the user to design, create, and publish a professional newsletter, newspaper, or class magazine; and paint programs provide the vehicle to digitize photos, create art, and use the imagination in ways previously not accessible to the classroom.

WHY TECHNOLOGY? *(cont.)*

Technology can also be a vehicle for expanding the teaching and learning methods used in your classroom. Perhaps you love doing large-group discussions and you're great at them, but you're not as comfortable with small group collaborative projects. How can technology help? There are software programs that are specifically designed for small groups that will actually help you create, sustain, and enjoy cooperative environments.

These type of programs are especially helpful in the one-computer classroom in which previously your only option was a management nightmare—rotating thirty students through one computer.

The Bottom Line

When thinking about technology use within any school and curricular area, it is important to remember that technology shouldn't take over your classroom or make things more difficult for you. Rather, it should be used to enhance and expand your classroom, make your life easier, and make your students' learning more meaningful.

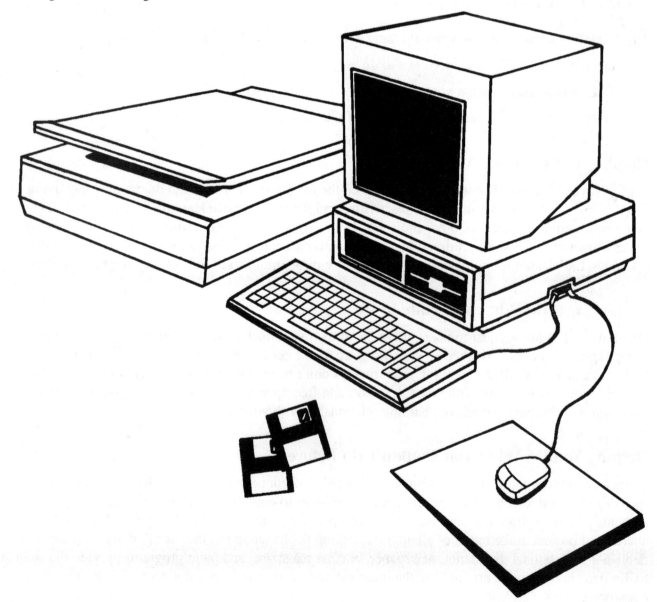

TYPES OF SOFTWARE

There are many methods to categorize computer software. The following categorization provides a structure that can make it easier to think about the kinds of programs that can be helpful in the classroom.

Word Processing

Word processing software allows you to put text into an electronic format that permits easy manipulation, editing, and publishing. The advantages of this software are many, including the ability to move blocks of text, edit, spell check, draft and rewrite, and design creative text layouts. Even newsletters can be generated using most word processing applications.

Database

Database software enables you to easily enter and store huge amounts of data and quickly access, manipulate, and run comparisons and correlations, statistical analyses, and cause/effect relationships. Databases are especially useful within the social studies curriculum.

Graph Programs

Graph programs enable you to easily and quickly create graphs, such as line, bar, table, circle, and picture graphs. Like database programs, graphing programs allow you to manipulate the data at the touch of a button and print out the results in full color.

Paint Programs

Paint programs enable you to create original art, as well as manipulate digitized photos, graphics, and other first-person documents and reference materials. Creations from your paint software can be imported into any of the programs described above.

Multimedia

Multimedia has been around far longer than the buzzword and has received a great deal of hype as a "new" way to use technology. However, the use of multiple media has been a part of the classroom since the beginning of education. The addition of the computer into schools has created this "new" category of multimedia. Computers allow you to incorporate several media into high-tech presentations with minimal programming skills. Programs such as *HyperStudio*, *Kid Pix 2*, *ClarisWorks*, and *Director* are popular examples of multimedia presentation tools. Keep in mind that if you lack these programs, a simple piece of word processing software hooked into a television or an LCD (liquid crystal display) panel can also be used to create excellent presentations.

Simulations

Simulations, like multimedia, have been a part of the classroom infrastructure for years. Computers, however, can make simulations easier. They can help manage large amounts of data, track students' progress, and create nonthreatening environments in which students can practice (over and over) their critical thinking and decision-making skills. Simulations can be used with an entire class at once, as well as help you manage small-group or role-playing activities.

TYPES OF SOFTWARE (cont.)

Drill and Practice

In the majority of schools, drill and practice is still the most popular use of the computer. This Skinnerian ideal is often nothing more than hi-tech flashcards. And, rotating thirty kids through one computer in forty-five minutes is no one's idea of a fun time. In spite of classroom management issues and the plethora of inappropriate software, there can be many beneficial and appropriate uses of single-computer software in both the classroom and lab settings.

Internet Applications

The latest and hottest technology term is the "information superhighway." Again, one must be cautious of the promising hype. There are many positive benefits of Internet access, but it is certainly not an all-encompassing panacea that will magically solve all educational problems. That said, applications such as e-mail and online researching can be tremendous assets to any classroom. The communication possibilities of the Internet are truly moving us towards a global village. And, an exciting-byproduct of hooking classrooms to the Internet is that finally more and more teachers are able to communicate with other educators.

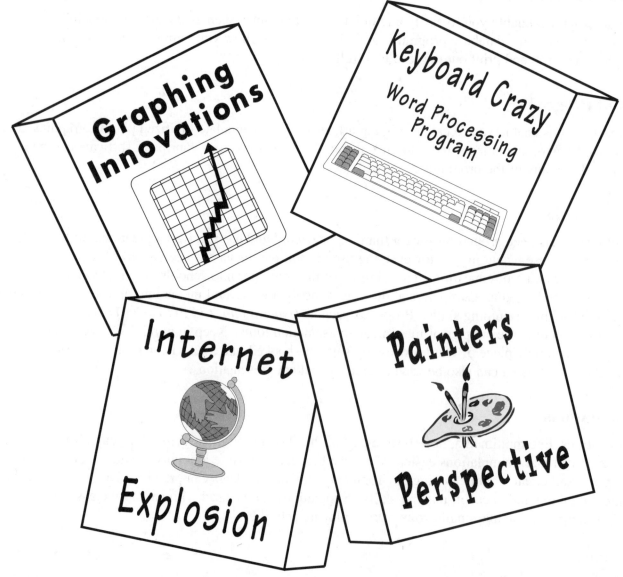

THE NATIONAL COUNCIL FOR THE SOCIAL STUDIES STANDARDS: NCSS

The activities in this book are presented within the framework of ten thematic units of the National Council for the Social Studies Standards. The following describes the reasoning behind these standards.

What is the purpose of the NCSS standards?

Our world is changing rapidly. Students in our schools today, who will be the citizens of the twenty-first century, are living and learning in the midst of a knowledge explosion unlike any humankind has ever experienced. Because schools and teachers cannot teach everything, and because students cannot learn all there is to know, the Council's document focuses on three purposes for the standards. The social studies standards should

1. serve as a framework for K–12 social studies program design through the use of ten thematic strands;
2. serve as a guide for curriculum decisions by providing performance expectations regarding knowledge, processes, and attitudes essential for all students; and
3. provide examples of classroom practice to guide teachers in designing instruction to help students meet performance expectations. These social studies standards provide criteria for making decisions as curriculum planners and teachers address such issues as why teach social studies, what to include in the curriculum, how to teach it well to all students, and how to assess whether or not students are able to apply what they have learned.

The ten thematic curriculum standards and accompanying sets of student performance expectations constitute an irreducible minimum of what is essential in social studies.

Along with the examples of classroom practice, these standards and performance expectations help answer the following questions:

- How can the social studies curriculum help students construct an accurate and positive view of citizenship and become citizens able to address persistent issues, promote civic ideals and practices, and improve our democratic republic?
- What content themes are essential to the curriculum at every level (early, middle, and high school) because they address societal expectations and the needs of young future citizens and are drawn from disciplines and fields related to social studies and from other disciplines and fields that are natural allies of social studies?
- What are the student performance expectations at early, middle, and high school levels for knowledge, skills, attitudes, civic ideals, and practices that encompass social studies as an integrative field?
- How can learning opportunities be structured at each school level to help students meet social studies performance expectations?
- How might performance expectations be assessed to show that students have constructed an understanding that allows them to demonstrate and apply what they have learned?

THEME 1
CULTURE

Social studies programs should include experiences that provide for the study of culture and cultural diversity. Human beings create, learn, and adapt culture. Culture helps us to understand ourselves as both individuals and members of various groups. Human cultures exhibit both similarities and differences. We all, for example, have systems of beliefs, knowledge, values, and traditions. Each system also is unique. In a democratic and multicultural society, students need to understand multiple perspectives that derive from different cultural vantage points.

This understanding will allow them to relate to people in our nation and throughout the world. Cultures are dynamic and ever-changing. The study of culture prepares students to ask and answer questions such as: What are the common characteristics of different cultures? How do belief systems, such as religion or political ideals of the culture, influence the other parts of the culture? How does the culture change to accommodate different ideas and beliefs? What does language tell us about the culture?

In schools, this theme typically appears in units and courses dealing with geography, history, and anthropology, as well as multicultural topics across the curriculum. During the early years of school, the exploration of the concepts of likenesses and differences in school subjects such as language arts, mathematics, science, music, and art makes the study of culture appropriate.

Socially, the young learner is beginning to interact with other students, some of whom are like the student and some different; naturally, he or she wants to know more about others. In the middle grades, students begin to explore and ask questions about the nature of culture and specific aspects of culture, such as language and beliefs, and the influence of those aspects on human behavior. As students progress through high school, they can understand and use complex cultural concepts such as adaptation, assimilation, acculturation, diffusion, and dissonance drawn from anthropology, sociology, and other disciplines to explain how culture and cultural systems function.

DEFINE A CULTURE

Culture affects who we are and how we think and act. In this lesson, students will research and discover the components and characteristics that make up cultures.

Grade Level: three to five

Duration: 30 minutes

Materials: CD-ROM multimedia encyclopedia; copies of "Define a Culture Work Sheet," pages 12 and 13

Procedure:

Before the Computer

- Have students individually write their own definitions of the word "culture."
- Next, create a whole-class definition of the word.
- Have students find definitions of "culture" in the dictionary.
- Discuss the different definitions.
- In small or large groups, have students brainstorm and generate a list of different cultures.
- Write these lists on the board and discuss them.
- Break the class into groups for CD-ROM research.

On the Computer

- Have students use the CD-ROM encyclopedia to research different cultures.

After the Computer

- Have students complete the "Define a Culture Work Sheet."

Option:

- Create a database with the information using *ClarisWorks, The Graph Club,* or a similar program. Run comparisons and correlations between the cultures.

DEFINE A CULTURE WORK SHEET

Name: _____   Date: _____

1. **To which culture do you belong?**

   _____

   _____

   _____

2. **List beliefs, values, and traditions of your culture.**

   _____

   _____

   _____

3. **What do you think all cultures have in common?**

   _____

   _____

   _____

4. **How do you become part of a culture?**

   _____

   _____

   _____

5. **Do you belong to more than one culture?**

   _____

   _____

   _____

6. **Is the sixth grade a culture?**

   _____

   _____

   _____

DEFINE A CULTURE WORK SHEET *(cont.)*

7. Are teachers a culture?

_____

_____

_____

_____

_____

8. Is yogurt a culture?

_____

_____

_____

_____

_____

9. What are the characteristics and traits of a culture (e.g., beliefs, values, traditions, . . .)?

_____

_____

_____

_____

_____

10. Create a collage that pulls together various elements of your culture such as photos of people, geography, food, art, music, etc.

RESEARCH A CULTURE

In this lesson students will apply their definitions to learning about specific cultures. Browsing the Internet, students will gather information regarding different cultures of the world.

Grade Level: three to five

Duration: 45 minutes

Materials: computer with Internet access; copies of "Research a Culture Work Sheet," page 15

Procedure:

Before the Computer

- On the chalkboard or computer, demonstrate how to perform a search on the Internet using search engines such as Yahoo!, Excite, AltaVista, or Netscape Navigator.

- Discuss the function of hyperlinks and URLs.

- Distribute the work sheet and review it with the class.

- Have students pick a culture for an Internet search.

- Review key search words that students might use for their searches, e.g., hippies, religion, fashion, ethnicity, politics, and generation X.

On the Computer

- Perform a Web search on the culture of choice.

- Be sure to check out multiple sites to increase variety and diversity.

- Complete the worksheet.

After the Computer

- List on the chalkboard cultural characteristics from the worksheets. (Save the list for the next lesson.)

Option:

- Research another culture.

RESEARCH A CULTURE WORK SHEET

Name: _____   Date: _____

1. List five characteristics that make this culture unique.

_____

_____

_____

_____

_____

2. How is this culture similar to yours?

_____

_____

_____

3. How is this culture different?

_____

_____

_____

4. In the box below draw symbols from this culture, flag, crest, logo, etc.

CREATE A CULTURE

In this project, students will create two-minute "infomercials" on their cultures of choice, using text, graphics, and sound.

Grade Level: three to five

Duration: three to five days

Materials: copies of "Create a Culture Work Sheet," page 17; video camera; multimedia equipment; print materials; poster board; completed work sheets from pages 12–13 and 15

Procedure:

Before the Computer

- Use the completed Define a Culture and Research a Culture Work Sheets to generate identifying characteristics of cultures.

- Have students work in groups to complete the "Create a Culture Work Sheet.

On the Computer

- Have students use *ClarisWorks* to create a slide show presentation of their newly developed culture. Or, they can use *HyperStudio* to create a multimedia presentation of their culture or *Kid Pix* to create a slide show. (See the *Kid Pix* Planning Sheet on page 132.) Another option is to have them create a video presentation/infomercial or use another appropriate presentation tool maker.

After the Computer

- Present the cultures to the class.

CREATE A CULTURE WORK SHEET

Name: _____   Date: _____

1. **Name the culture** _____

2. **List the culture's traits**

   _____

   _____

   _____

   _____

   _____

3. **Create a flag.**

4. **Create a logo/crest.**

5. **Write a *We Believe* . . . poem. Here is an example.**

   We believe democracy is cool.

   We believe creamy peanut butter is cool.

   We believe animals have feelings.

6. **Prepare a sample menu of the foods particular to your culture.**

7. **Create an anthem for your culture.**

8. **List major traditions, rituals, ceremonies, and customs of your culture.**

   _____

   _____

   _____

   _____

   _____

   _____

SEARCHING ON THE INTERNET

Directions: First, go to your favorite search engine or use one of the search engines listed below. Then use the keywords and phrases to locate Web sites for your project.

AltaVista	*http://www.altavista.com*
Excite	*http://www.excite.com*
Hotbot	*http://www.hotbot.com*
Lycos	*http://www.lycos.com*
Yahoo!	*http://www.yahoo.com*
Profusion	*http://www.profusion.com*

Keywords and Phrases

"Africa Online"

Artists (Try the Yahoo subject lists to retrieve a long list of artists)

"Black History" or "African American History"

CIA or "CIA Factbook"

"Discovery Channel"

"Diverse Cultures"

Earth

"Ellis Island"

"Global Education"

"Historical Text Archive"

"History Channel"

Hyperhistory

"Interactive Atlas"

MapQuest

Museums or "Museum Hotlist"

Peacecorps

"Primary Historical Documents"

"Renaissance or Enlightenment"

Theater

"United Nations"

"World Communities" or "Ethnic Groups"

PROGRAMS

- *ABC NewsLinks*—Creative Wonders
- *AfricaTrail*—The Learning Company
- *Decisions, Decisions: Prejudice*—Tom Snyder Productions
- *Cultural Debates*—Tom Snyder Productions
- *TimeLiner*—Tom Snyder Productions
- *MayaQuest*—The Learning Company
- *Totem Poles*—Diatech
- *If Monks Had Macs*—Voyager
- *American Muse*—Voyager
- *Religions of the World*—Mentorom
- *Strategy Games of the World*—Edmark
- *World Beat*—Medio
- *History and Culture Of*—Queue
- *Introduction to Archeology*—Queue
- *The Face of Life*—Creative Multimedia
- *American Indian Encyclopedia*—Facts on File
- *Reel Women*—Enteractive
- *The Story of Civilization*—Flagtower
- *History of the World*—Dorling Kindersley
- *Chronicle of the 20th Century*—Dorling Kindersley
- *Mythology*—Thomas S. Klise
- *Makers of the 20th Century*—News Multimedia
- *The Clothes We Wore*—E.M.M.E.
- *Origins of Mankind*—Maris
- *The Silk Road*—DNA Multimedia
- *World Book Encyclopedia*—Grolier
- *Bartlett's Familiar Quotations*—Time Warner

THEME 2
TIME, CONTINUITY, AND CHANGE

Social studies programs should include experiences that provide for the study of the ways human beings view themselves in and over time. Human beings seek to understand their historical roots and to locate themselves in time. Such understanding involves knowing what things were like in the past and how things change and develop. Knowing how to read and reconstruct the past allows one to develop a historical perspective and to answer questions such as: Who am I? What happened in the past? How am I connected to those in the past? How has the world changed and how might it change in the future? Why does our personal sense of relatedness to the past change? How can the perspective we have about our own life experiences be viewed as part of the larger human story across time? How do our personal stories reflect varying points of view and inform contemporary ideas and actions? This theme typically appears in courses that

1. include perspectives from various aspects of history,

2. draw upon historical knowledge during the examination of social issues, and

3. develop the habits of mind that historians and scholars in the humanities and social sciences employ to study the past and its relationship to the present in the United States and other societies.

Learners in early grades gain experience with sequencing to establish a sense of order and time. They enjoy hearing stories of the recent past as well as of long ago. In addition, they begin to recognize that individuals may hold different views about the past and to understand the linkages between human decisions and consequences. Thus, the foundation is laid for the development of historical knowledge, skills, and values.

In the middle grades, students, through a more formal study of history, continue to expand their understanding of the past and of historical concepts and inquiry. They begin to understand and appreciate differences in historical perspectives, recognizing that interpretations are influenced by individual experiences, societal values, and cultural traditions.

High school students engage in more sophisticated analysis and reconstruction of the past, examining its relationship to the present and extrapolating into the future. They integrate individual stories about people, events, and situations to form a more holistic conception in which continuity and change are linked in time and across cultures. Students also learn to draw on their knowledge of history to make informed choices and decisions in the present.

YOUR BIRTHDAY THROUGH HISTORY

In this lesson, students will establish and understand their place in history by researching key events that occurred on their birthday throughout history. Linking their birthdays to key historical events and highlighting important events and people who have come before them provides a context for examining continuity of time.

Grade Level: three to five

Duration: 45 minutes

Materials: copies of "Your Birthday Through History Work Sheet," page 22; computer with Internet access; library; CD-ROM encyclopedia; microfilm or microfiche of past newspapers and magazines

Procedure:

Before the Computer

- Explain to the students that they will be researching different periods in history. More specifically, they will be picking events throughout history that occurred on their birth dates. For example, if a student was born January 22, 1988, he or she could research the following dates: 1/22/1997, 1/22/1970, 1/22/1945, 1/22/1959, 1/22/1492, 1/22/1776, 1/22/1961, and 1/22/1975.

On the Computer

- Have students enter their information into a database program.
- Make a time line of these events on construction paper or use the program *TimeLiner* by Tom Snyder Productions, combining the entire class' events.

After the Computer

- Make a classroom newspaper, for example *The Daily Century,* that includes articles of the key events generated from the search.

YOUR BIRTHDAY THROUGH HISTORY WORK SHEET

Name: _____   Date: _____

Date _____

Event _____

Place _____

How did/does this event directly or indirectly affect your life?

_____

_____

_____

_____

Date _____

Event _____

Place _____

How did/does this event directly or indirectly affect your life?

_____

_____

_____

_____

Date _____

Event _____

Place _____

How did/does this event directly or indirectly affect your life?

_____

_____

_____

YOUR HISTORICAL BIRTHDAY TWIN

In this lesson, students will each research an historical figure who was born on the same month and day as they were. They will compare the historical figure's life to their own.

Grade Level: three to five

Duration: three hours

Materials: copies of your "Historical Birthday Twin Work Sheet," page 23; Internet access; CD-ROM encyclopedia; newspaper and magazine microfilm

Procedure:

Before the Computer

- Distribute the "Historical Birthday Twin Worksheet."
- Be sure students are proficient in performing Internet searches.

On the Computer

- Using the work sheet as a guide, have students begin their research.
- Have students each perform a search on their birthdays (month and day) for random years throughout history until they find a famous figure who shares their birthday and or whom they want to report.

After the Computer

- Have students write reports on their birthday twins. They can dress up as the characters and present first-person narratives about their lives.

YOUR HISTORICAL BIRTHDAY TWIN WORK SHEET

Name: _____   Date: _____

Name of person with your birthdate _____

Time period person lived/lives _____

Accomplishments

_____

_____

_____

_____

Similarities to you

_____

_____

_____

_____

Differences from you

_____

_____

_____

_____

Name ways this person has influenced history

_____

_____

_____

_____

CORRELATIONS IN TIME

Within this activity students will learn how social and economic events are related. By creating databases and tracking parallels, they will see how these two important historical and topical forces shape and drive each other.

Grade Level: three to five

Duration: ongoing

Materials: copies of "Correlations Work Sheet," page 26; database software; word processing software; Internet access

Procedure:

Before the Computer

- Divide your class into four groups.

- Explain to the class that they will be creating a database to examine positive or negative correlations between historical events and social phenomena.

- Provide sample correlations to students, such as: "How did the growth of railroads in the late 1800s affect the unemployment rate?" or "What happened to inflation during wartimes?"

- Using the worksheet, each group will collect data on one or more of the following topics, or other topics they choose, between a specific time period:

employment	welfare
railroad expansion	immigration
natural disasters	population
political trends	wars
epidemics	inflation

On the Computer

- Use CD-ROM, Internet, encyclopedias, or other reference materials to collect quantifiable data on the above topics within the specified time period.

- Use database programs such as: *Access* (Microsoft), *Approach* (Lotus), *Paradox* (Borland) to input the data.

- Run correlations between any two topics. For example, is there a positive correlation between natural disasters and a fall in population?

- Create graphs. Print and discuss.

CORRELATIONS WORK SHEET

Group Members: _____   Date: _____

_____

_____

Research meaningful topics and collect statistical data over time on several topics. Input this data into a database to run correlations.

Subject	Date Start	Date End	Pertinent Information

GRANDPARENTS

This activity provides a platform for students to identify and isolate social and technological changes and advances over time by comparing the past with the present via interviews. Based on this data students will make predictions about the future.

Grade Level: three to five

Duration: two hours

Materials: copies of "Interviewing Relatives Work Sheet," page 28; handheld digital recorder; notebook; tape recorder

Procedure:

- Help students make a list of all the activities they do before coming to school. For example, brushing hair, brushing teeth, eating breakfast, putting on clothes, driving to school, etc.

- List the technologies and mechanical devices used to accomplish these activities. Some examples include hairbrush, toothbrush, toaster, automobile, gas or electric stove, microwave.

- Have students interview grandparents or other older relatives and ask them how they started their day when they were the students' age. What were their activities? What were the available technologies?

- Compare the technologies. How did things change? How did they stay the same? Why do you think they changed?

- Pretend it's fifty-plus years in the future and your grandchild comes home with this some assignment. How will the activities differ?

Options

- Use *Paintshop Pro, ClarisWorks,* or another paint program to design a product students think will be in widespread use in 2053. Examples could include the microwave flyswatter or the telephone handset blow-dryer combo.

INTERVIEWING RELATIVES WORK SHEET

Date:_____

Interviewer: _____

Interviewee: _____

Technologies used to start the day:

_____

_____

_____

_____

_____

Compared to now, was life easier or harder then? Why?

_____

_____

_____

_____

_____

Additional information:

_____

_____

_____

_____

_____

PAST PRESIDENTS

Students learn about the complexity of current social issues by examining the past political platforms of presidents prior to the 1900s.

Grade Level: three to five

Duration: 20–40 minutes

Materials: copies of "Past Presidents Work Sheet," page 30; word processing software; Internet access; CD-ROM encyclopedia; camcorder

Procedure:

Before the Computer

- Pick a president in office prior to 1900 and research his political philosophy and platforms. For example: George Washington on women's rights or Abraham Lincoln on gun control.

- Do the past political solutions apply to today's issues? If so, how? If not, why not?

- Pick five current political issues such as welfare, health care, education, censorship, TV and movie ratings.

On the Computer

- Create a multimedia presentation or television commercial on what that past president's platform would be on one or more of today's issues.

After the Computer

- Share the presentations with other classes.

Option:

- Post the presentations on the Internet for other schools to visit.

PAST PRESIDENTS WORK SHEET

Name: _____   Date: _____

President: _____

Dates in Office: _____

Presidential Party: _____

Description of Presidential Platform

_____

_____

_____

_____

_____

Current Political Issue:

_____

_____

_____

_____

_____

How do you think this president would resolve this current issue?

_____

_____

_____

_____

_____

SEARCHING ON THE INTERNET

Directions: First, go to your favorite search engine or use one of the search engines listed below. Then use the keywords and phrases to locate Web sites for your project.

AltaVista	*http://www.altavista.com*
Excite	*http://www.excite.com*
Hotbot	*http://www.hotbot.com*
Lycos	*http://www.lycos.com*
Yahoo!	*http://www.yahoo.com*
Profusion	*http://www.profusion.com*

Keywords and Phrases

"Almanac of Birthdays"

"American Immigration"

"American Memory"

"America's Presidential Libraries"

"Daily Almanac"

"Early American Archives"

"Election Results"

"Global Education"

Grolier

"Historical Text Archive"

Historyplace

Hyperhistory

"Library of Congress"

"Museum Hotlist"

"National Archives"

"Newspapers in Education"

PBS

Reconstruction

"Revolutionary War"

"Revolutionary War Time Line"

"United States History"

"World Factbook"

PROGRAMS

- *Family Gathering*—Palladium

- *Family Tree Maker*—Broderbund

- *TimeLiner*—Tom Snyder Productions

- *The Ripple that Changed American History*—Tom Snyder Productions

- *Point of View*—Scholastic

- *Time Treks*—Sanctuary Woods

- *Chronos*—Tom Snyder Productions

- *World Book Encyclopedia*—Grolier

- *CD Source Book of American History*—Compact University

- *Our Secret Century: The Darker Side of Our Collective Past*—Voyager

- *The Story of Civilization*—World Library

- *Flagtower 20th Century*—Flagtower

THEME 3
PEOPLE, PLACES, AND ENVIRONMENT

Social studies programs should include experiences that provide for the study of people, places, and environments. Technological advances connect students at all levels to the world beyond their personal locations. The study of people, places, and human-environment interactions assists learners as they create their spatial views and geographic perspectives of the world.

Today's social, cultural, economic, and civic demands on individuals mean that students will need the knowledge, skills, and understanding to ask and answer questions such as: Where are things located? Why are they located where they are? What patterns are reflected in the groupings of things? What do we mean by region? How do landforms change? What implications do these changes have for people? This area of study helps learners make informed and critical decisions about the relationships between human beings and their environments. In schools, this theme typically appears in units and courses dealing with area studies and geography.

In the early grades, young learners draw upon immediate personal experiences as a basis for exploring geographic concepts and skills. They also express interest in things distant and unfamiliar and have concern for the use and abuse of the physical environment.

During the middle school years, students relate their personal experiences to happenings in other environmental contexts. Appropriate experiences will encourage increasingly abstract thought as students use data and apply skills in analyzing human behavior in relation to its physical and cultural environment.

Students in high school are able to apply geographic understanding across a broad range of fields, including the fine arts, sciences, and humanities. Geographic concepts become central to learners' comprehension of global connections as they expand their knowledge of diverse cultures, both historical and contemporary. The importance of core geographic themes to public policy is recognized and should be explored as students address issues of domestic and international significance.

MONTAGE HOUSE MAP

This is the first of a three-part mapping project. The activities begin with a personal exploration and then progress to exploring students' community and then world. This exercise helps students understand the complex nature of "environment." Students begin abstract explorations of their environments with concrete investigations and studies of their homes.

Grade Level: three to five

Duration: two to three hours

Materials: computer, scanner, items from students' homes

Procedure:

Before the Computer

- Discuss the functions and meanings of personal symbols and icons.
- Have students bring in small items, photos, or pictures that represent each room of their houses.

On the Computer

- Scan the items into computer. Have students create a photo montage layouts of their houses.

After the Computer

- Print out photo montages of their houses and have students explain the significance of each icon and/or photo.

Option:

- Redesign your house with possible new icons you would like to add to your personal montage. Why would you make the changes you did?

NEIGHBORHOOD MAP MONTAGE

In this project students continue to explore their environment by creating a map of their neighborhoods.

Grade Level: three to five

Duration: two to three hours

Materials: computer and scanner

Procedure:

Before the Computer

- On the blackboard or computer, demonstrate to the students how to sketch a map by drawing a map of the school or other familar site. Discuss the functions of symbols, compass rose, and the key. Go over the directions so that they clearly understand the assignment. Their hand-drawn maps will serve as the basis for their computer generated maps.

At the Computer

- Using a mapping program like *Neighborhood Map Machine* (Tom Snyder Productions) or a paint program like *Kid Pix* (Broderbund), have the students recreate their hand-drawn maps. Make sure that they include a key and symbols.

After the Computer

- Print the maps and display them in class.

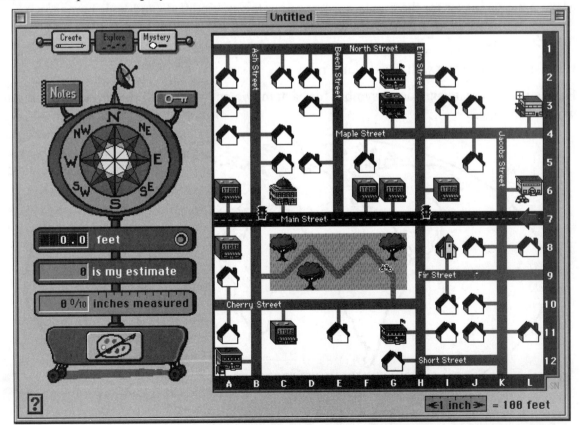

STAR MAPS

In this third and final lesson of the map series, students explore exotic locations and their relationship to their home towns via their favorite movies.

Grade Level: three to five

Duration: 45 minutes

Materials: computer with Internet access, word processing software, paint program

Procedure:

Before the Computer

- Explain this activity to your students so they understand it.
- With your students, make a list of current films that take place in different countries.
- Divide students into appropriate groups.
- Have each group select a film.
- Create a map with directions how to get to that country from your classroom. For example, *Seven Years in Tibet,* starring Brad Pitt, was filmed in Tibet.

On the Computer

- Look up the Web site of the movie.
- Make a movie poster for the movie, incorporating the exotic locale and your home town.

After the Computer

- Have students create a wall-sized world map.
- Have students create an icon or symbol for each movie and paste it to the proper location on the world wall map.

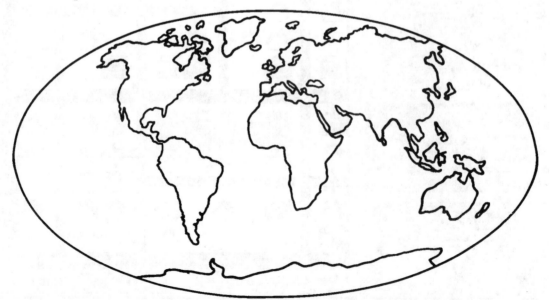

ETHNIC RESTAURANTS

Students explore the cultural diversity of their environment by interviewing local owners of ethnic restaurants.

Grade Level: three to five

Duration: 45 minutes

Materials: copies of "Ethnic Restaurants Work Sheet," page 38;"tape recorder; notepad; spreadsheet program

Procedure:

Before the Computer

- Discuss issues related to cultural diversity and ethnicity.

- Generate a list of questions that can be used in the interview process along with the Ethnic Restaurants Work Sheet on the next page.

- Have students interview restaurant owners. Where they are from? How did they get there? Generate more questions on your own.

On the Computer

- Create a multimedia presentation on the differences and similarities among the different ethnicities.

Options:

- Have an ethnic food day in your class.

ETHNIC RESTAURANTS WORK SHEET

Interviewer: _____   Date: _____

Interviewee: _____

1. Where are you from?

   _____

2. How did you get to this country?

   _____

   _____

3. Why did you move here?

   _____

   _____

4. What do you miss about your native country?

   _____

   _____

5. What do you like about this country?

   _____

   _____

6. What are some differences between America and your birth country?

   _____

   _____

7. What is your favorite food?

   _____

8. What represents American food to you?

   _____

9. Add more questions here:

   _____

   _____

   _____

SEARCHING ON THE INTERNET

Directions: First, go to your favorite search engine or use one of the search engines listed below. Then use the keywords and phrases to locate Web sites for your project.

AltaVista	*http://www.altavista.com*
Excite	*http://www.excite.com*
Hotbot	*http://www.hotbot.com*
Lycos	*http://www.lycos.com*
Yahoo!	*http://www.yahoo.com*
Profusion	*http://www.profusion.com*

Keywords and Phrases

"Almanac of Birthdays"

Artists(Try the Yahoo subject lists to retrieve a long list of artists)

"Cultural Diversity"

"Daily Almanac"

"Democracy in Schools"

EdWeb AND Democracy

Enlightenment

"Historical Text Archive"

"History Channel"

Hyperhistory

"Interactive Atlas"

MapQuest

Museums or "Museum Hotlist"

Renaissance

"United States History"

"World History"

PROGRAMS

- *Time Multimedia Almanac*—Softkey
- *SimTower*—Maxis
- *SimTown*—Maxis
- *SimCity*—Maxis
- *Family Gathering*—Palladium
- *Where In The World*—Broderbund
- *Maps 'N' Facts*—Broderbund
- *Physical World*—Mentorom
- *Land & Air*—Mentorom
- *Water*—Mentorom
- *Small Blue Planet*—Cambrix
- *3D Atlas*—Electronic Arts
- *Cartopedia*—Dorling Kindersley
- *World Discovery*—Great Wave
- *Map & Go*—Delorme
- *Volcanoes*—Corbis
- *Encarta World Atlas*—Microsoft
- *Skytrip America*—Discovery Channel
- *Exploring Yellowstone*—MECC
- *Quick Reference Atlas*—Rand McNally
- *World Atlas*—Mindscape
- *World Vista*—Applied Optical Media
- *American Vista*—Applied Optical Media
- *Travelrama USA*—Sanctuary Woods
- *Geography Search*—Tom Snyder Productions
- *Decisions, Decisions: The Environment*—Tom Sndyer Productions
- *Neighborhood Map Machine*—Tom Sndyer Productions
- *National Inspirer*—Tom Sndyer Productions
- *Mapping the World by Heart*—Tom Sndyer Productions
- *Her Heritage: Famous American Women*—Pilgrim New Media
- *The Story of Civilization*—World Library
- *Origins of Mankind: 70 Million Years of Content*—Maris

THEME 4
INDIVIDUAL DEVELOPMENT AND IDENTITY

Social studies programs should include experiences that provide for the study of individual development and identity. Personal identity is shaped by one's culture, by groups, and by institutional influences. How do people learn? Why do people behave as they do? What influences how people learn, perceive, and grow? How do people meet their basic needs in a variety of contexts? Questions such as these are central to the study of how individuals develop from youth to adulthood.

Examination of various forms of human behavior enhances understanding of the relationships among social norms and emerging personal identities, the social processes that influence identity formation, and the ethical principles underlying individual action. In schools, this theme typically appears in units and courses dealing with psychology and anthropology. Given the nature of individual development and our own cultural context, students need to be aware of the processes of learning, growth, and development at every level of their school experience.

In the early grades, for example, observing brothers, sisters, and older adults, looking at family photo albums, remembering past achievements and projecting oneself into the future, and comparing the patterns of behavior evident in people of different age groups are appropriate activities because young learners develop their personal identities in the context of families, peers, schools, and communities. Central to this development are the exploration, identification, and analysis of how individuals relate to others.

In the middle grades, issues of personal identity are refocused as the individual begins to explain self in relation to others in the society and culture.

At the high school level, students need to encounter multiple opportunities to examine contemporary patterns of human behavior, using methods from the behavioral sciences to apply core concepts drawn from psychology, social psychology, sociology, and anthropology as they apply to individuals, societies, and cultures.

PERSONAL TIME LINE

Picking key events in their lives helps students define who they are today. This activity provides a structure for this definition.

Grade Level: three to five

Duration: two to four hours

Materials: copies of "Personal Events Work Sheet," page 43; *TimeLiner* software; butcher paper

Procedure:

Before the Computer

- Have students reflect on their lives and pick important events and people who influenced them.
- Distribute and have students complete the Personal Events Work Sheet.

On the Computer

- Using *TimeLiner* by Tom Snyder Productions, or another sequencing program, enter the events to create a time line.
- Or, create a time line using butcher paper.
- Examine how events and people shaped your life.

After the Computer

- Print time lines.
- Merge time lines to see the relative influence of people on events and vice versa.

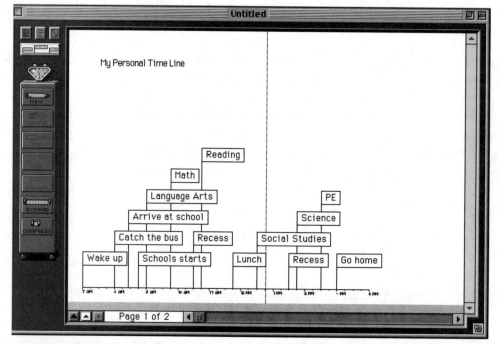

From Tom Snyder Production's *TimeLiner* 4.0

PERSONAL EVENTS WORK SHEET

Name: _____   Date: _____

Significant Event or Person

Person: _____

Event: _____

Date event occurred:_____

How it changed me. (Why this event was significant.)

_____

_____

_____

_____

Significant Event or Person

Person: _____

Event: _____

Date event occurred:_____

How it changed me. (Why this event was significant.)

_____

_____

_____

_____

Significant Event or Person

Person: _____

Event: _____

Date event occurred:_____

How it changed me. (Why this event was significant.)

_____

_____

_____

_____

FAMILY TREE MAKER

Students research their family history by interviewing their parents and grandparents and then create a family tree using a paint or family tree program.

Grade Level: three to five

Duration: two to four hours

Materials: copies of "Family Tree Questionnaire," page 45; paint program; tape recorder

Procedure:

Before the Computer

- Be sure your class has a firm understanding of the concept of genealogy and the process of creating a family tree.

- Use the Family Tree Questionnaire to generate questions to ask in your interviews.

- Have students interview family members.

On the Computer

- Have students use a paint program to design and create a family tree.

Options

- Design a family crest for your family tree.

- Create an imaginary family tree.

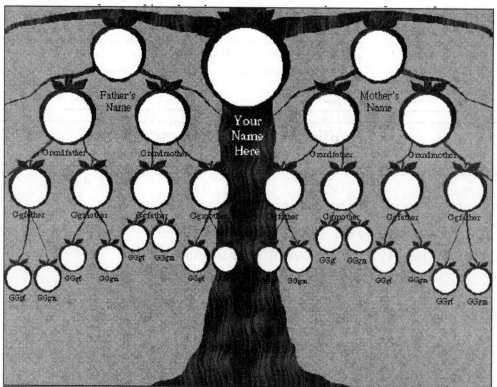

FAMILY TREE QUESTIONNAIRE

Name: _____   Date: _____

1. Name of person being interviewed_____

2. Relationship of person to you_____

3. Country of birth_____

4. Native language_____

Add your own questions here.

5. _____

_____

6. _____

_____

7. _____

_____

8. _____

_____

9. _____

_____

10. _____

_____

11. _____

_____

12. _____

_____

13. _____

_____

WHAT'S YOUR SIGN?

Through this experience students study characteristics and traits that contribute to one's identity. This activity provides a vehicle for students to begin to explore and understand the many factors that make us who we are.

Grade Level: three to five

Duration: two hours

Materials: word processing or desktop publishing software with paint and draw capabilities, or paint and draw program software with word processing capabilities; Internet access

Procedure:

Before the Computer

- Divide the class into twelve groups according to their astrological signs.

- Have students investigate to find out the backgrounds of each of the signs. Research the mythology regarding the signs. Let them find out how this has influenced what characteristics are considered common to that sign. For example, Mars, connected with the sign Aries, appears to be red and so it has been associated with temper and aggression.

On the Computer

- Using word processing or desktop publishing software with paint and draw capabilities. or paint and draw program software with word processing capabilities, have each group create a picture of their astrological sign. They should label it with the name of the character represented and the dates.

Option:

- Combine the students work into a class book.

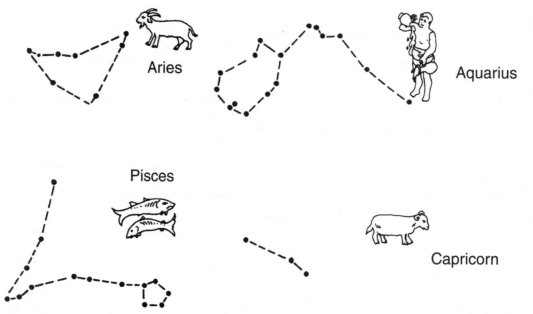

Aries

Aquarius

Pisces

Capricorn

INTERNET TWINS

What's in a name? Students will conduct a global search on the Net for people with the same name. (They will find many!) Through this experience students study characteristics and traits that make up one's identity, look for commonalities and differences, and continue to discuss how we acquire these characteristics.

Grade Level: three to five

Duration: two hours

Materials: copies of "Internet Twin Work Sheet," page 48; Internet access

Procedure:

Before the Computer

- Hand out the Internet Twin Work Sheet.

- Have students each generate a list of five questions pertaining to personal habits/tastes to ask their "identical" twins.

On the Computer

- Using the Internet, perform a global search on each student's name.

- Obtain the e-mail address of on identical twin.

- Using an e-mail program, send a questionnaire to the twin.

After the Computer

- Compare your tastes/habits to those of your twin. Are they similar? different? How do you explain this?

Option:

- Use the above exercise to segue into a discussion of genetic traits.

INTERNET TWINS WORK SHEET

Name: _____   Date: _____

Start with the following questions and then generate your own.

1. My favorite food is_____. What's yours?
2. I have _____ family members. How many do you have?
3. I can/can't curl my tongue. Can you?
4. My eyes are_____. What color are yours?

5. _____
   _____

6. _____
   _____

7. _____
   _____

8. _____
   _____

9. _____
   _____

10. _____
    _____

11. _____
    _____

12. _____
    _____

13. _____
    _____

14. _____
    _____

15. _____
    _____

SEARCHING ON THE INTERNET

Directions: First, go to your favorite search engine or use one of the search engines listed below. Then use the keywords and phrases to locate Web sites for your project.

AltaVista	*http://www.altavista.com*
Excite	*http://www.excite.com*
Hotbot	*http://www.hotbot.com*
Lycos	*http://www.lycos.com*
Yahoo!	*http://www.yahoo.com*
Profusion	*http://www.profusion.com*

Keywords and Phrases

"Almanac of Birthdays"

"American Immigration"

Artists(Try the Yahoo subject lists to retrieve a long list of artists)

"Asian American"

"Benjamin Franklin"

Biography.com

Black History" or "African American History"

"California Council for the Social Studies" (CCSS)

"Chicano Network"

"Cultural Diversity"

"Daily Almanac"

"Ellis Island"

Grolier

"Library of Congress"

"Native Americans"

"Native Web"

"Presidential Inaugural Addresses"

Unicef

"United States History"

PROGRAMS

- *Family Gathering*—Palladium

- *Family Tree Maker*—Broderbund

- *Time Multimedia Almanac*—Softkey

- *Origins of the Constitution*—Clearvue

- *The Face of Life*—Creative Multimedia

- *Landmark Documents in American History*—Facts on File

- *Grolier's Encyclopedia*

- *American Heritage Talking Dictionary*—American Heritage

- *TimeLiner*—Tom Snyder Productions

- *Neighborhood Map Machine*—Tom Snyder Productions

- *Ultimate Children's Encyclopedia*—Learning Company

- *Choices, Choices—On the Playground*—Tom Snyder Productions

- *Knowledge Quest Essentials*—C.B.E. Services

- *150 Years of Americas*—MacMillan Digital

- *Her Heritage: Famous American Women*—Pilgrim New Media

- *The Story of Civilization*—World Library

- *Origins of Mankind: 70 Million Years of Content*—Maris

THEME 5
INDIVIDUALS, GROUPS, AND INSTITUTIONS

Social studies programs should include experiences that provide for the study of interactions among individuals, groups, and institutions. Institutions such as schools, churches, families, government agencies, and the courts all play an integral role in our lives. These and other institutions exert enormous influence over us, yet, institutions are no more than organizational embodiments to further the core social values of those who comprise them.

Thus, it is important that students know how institutions are formed, what controls and influences them, how they control and influence individuals and culture, and how institutions can be maintained or changed. The study of individuals, groups, and institutions, drawing upon sociology, anthropology, and other disciplines, prepares students to ask and answer questions such as: What is the role of institutions in this and other societies? How am I influenced by institutions? How do institutions change? What is my role in institutional change? In schools, this theme typically appears in units and courses dealing with sociology, anthropology, psychology, political science, and history.

Young children should be given opportunities to examine various institutions that affect their lives and influence their thinking. They should be assisted in recognizing the tensions that occur when the goals, values, and principles of two or more institutions or groups conflict—for example, when the school board prohibits candy machines in schools vs. a class project to install a candy machine to help raise money for the local hospital. They should also have opportunities to explore ways in which institutions such as churches or health care networks are created to respond to changing individual and group needs.

Middle school learners will benefit from varied experiences through which they examine the ways in which institutions change over time, promote social conformity, and influence culture. They should be encouraged to use this understanding to suggest ways to work through institutional change for the common good.

High school students must understand the paradigms and traditions that undergird social and political institutions. They should be provided opportunities to examine, use, and add to the body of knowledge related to the behavioral sciences and social theory as it relates to the ways people and groups organize themselves around common needs, beliefs, and interests.

REINVENTING THE CLUB

Students examine the "clubs" or groups to which they belong and study the influence these organizations have on their lives.

Grade Level: three to five

Duration: one hour

Materials: copies of "Reinventing the Club Work Sheet," page 53; database software

Procedure:

Before the Computer

- Discuss the importance of belonging to a club or group with your students.

- Have students list the clubs to which they belong.

- Pass out the Reinventing the Club Work Sheet and have students complete it. Use page 54 to brainstorm about club activities, different leadership roles, purposes and goals, etc.

On the Computer

- Each student enters his or her data into a database.

- Compare and discuss.

- Answer questions such as:

    What are the most popular clubs and groups?

    What type of clubs are we born into?

    What are the advantages of belonging to a club or group?

    What are the disadvantages?

    What are the reasons for clubs?

    List the reasons for specific clubs?

    Why are some clubs exclusive?

    Should exclusivity be allowed?

    Why are clubs important?

After the Computer

- Discuss the results of the database comparisons and their significance.

REINVENTING THE CLUB WORK SHEET

Name: _____   Date: _____

Name of Group or Club	Description	Membership Requirements	Voluntary/ Mandatory

REINVENTING THE CLUB
WORK SHEET *(cont.)*

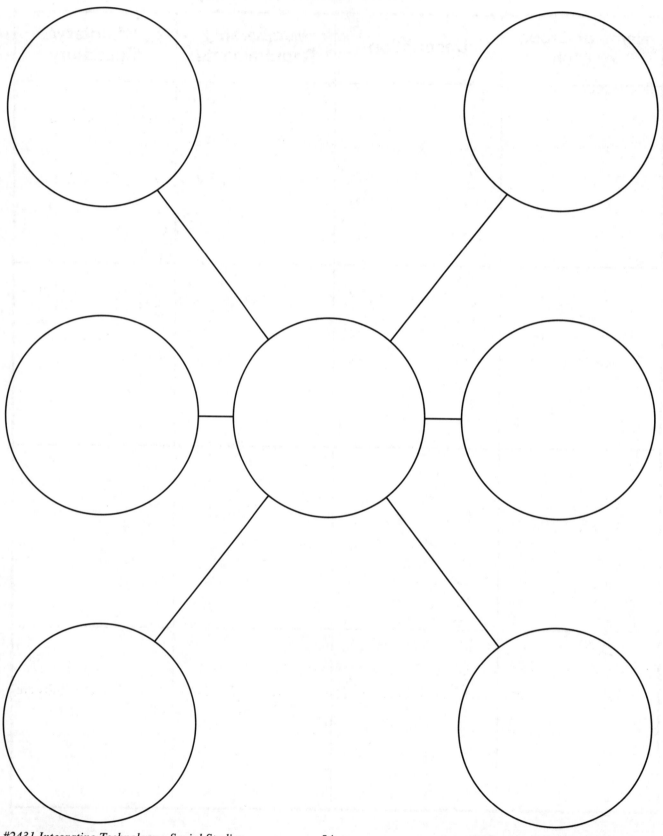

MEMBERSHIP

In this activity students will examine group psychology by creating an exclusive club. More specifically, students will work in groups, create clubs, and then try to recruit other classmates to join their clubs.

Grade Level: three to five

Duration: two hours

Materials: copies of "Create a Club Work Sheet," page 56, and "Club Propaganda Work Sheet," page 57; paint program such as *Photoshop*; presentation, multimedia, or slideshow software; VCR

Procedure:

Before the Computer

- Divide the class into groups.

- Each group creates a club using the Create a Club Work sheet.

- Using incentives, membership cards, and other propaganda, each group tries to recruit as many members as they can.

- Each group gives a multimedia, slide/show, video, or audio presentation to "sell" their club to their classmates.

- Emphasize that each student can belong to only one club at a time.

On the Computer

- Create membership cards.

- Create a group newsletter for the club.

- Create a group motto.

- Create a group song.

- Create a presentation.

After the Computer

- Have each group present its club.

- Pass out and complete the Club Propaganda Work Sheet.

- Have students design a method for tracking and tallying club membership.

- Discuss why some groups and clubs are popular while others are not; discuss why some clubs are exclusive and others are inclusive.

CREATE A CLUB WORK SHEET

Group Members: _____   Date: _____

_____

_____

Name of our club _____

Purpose

_____

_____

_____

_____

Motto

_____

_____

_____

_____

Logo

_____

_____

_____

_____

Design of membership card

CLUB PROPAGANDA WORK SHEET

Group Members: _____   Date: _____

_____

_____

Use this work sheet to create a newsletter to recruit members. Give three reasons why our club is better than all the other clubs:

1. _____

_____

_____

_____

_____

_____

2. _____

_____

_____

_____

_____

_____

_____

3. _____

_____

_____

_____

_____

_____

WIDGET WORLD, INC.

Students will experience the interactions and frictions among individuals, groups, and institutions by creating and developing a mock company. This ongoing activity divides your class into three group, workers, management, and board of directors of a company, and forces them to explore the dynamics of interelated groups within a company.

Grade Level: three to five

Duration: ongoing

Materials: copies of work sheets on pages 59–63, word processing software or paint program

Procedure:

Before the Computer

- Divide the class into three groups: workers, management, and board of directors.

- Be sure your students have a working understanding of these three groups. What are their motivations? What are their hopes and dreams? What differentiates them from each other? How are they similar? How do they usually interact?

- Have each group fill out their Widget Work Sheet and complete it from the group's perspective.

On the Computer

- Use a word processing software or paint program to create your group's version of the Widget Company Manifesto.

After the Computer

- After each group completes their group work sheet they must complete the Dispute and Reconciliation Work Sheet and come together as an entire company and complete the final Widget Company Manifesto Work Sheet.

WIDGET WORK SHEET: BOARD OF DIRECTORS

Group Members: _____   Date: _____

_____

_____

Complete the work sheet from the perspective of a member of the board of directors of Widget, Inc.

1. Mission Statement

   _____

   _____

   _____

2. Company Philosophy

   _____

   _____

   _____

3. Rules & Regulations

   _____

   _____

   _____

4. Employee Benefits

   _____

   _____

   _____

WIDGET WORK SHEET: MANAGEMENT

Group Members: _____   Date: _____

_____

_____

Complete the work sheet from your perspective as a manager of Widget, Inc.

1. Mission Statement

_____

_____

_____

_____

2. Company Philosophy

_____

_____

_____

_____

3. Rules & Regulations

_____

_____

_____

_____

4. Employee Benefits

_____

_____

_____

_____

WIDGET WORK SHEET: WORKERS

Group Members: _____   Date: _____

_____

_____

Complete the work sheet from your perspective as a worker of Widget, Inc.

1. Mission Statement

_____

_____

_____

2. Company Philosophy

_____

_____

_____

3. Rules & Regulations

_____

_____

_____

_____

4. Employee Benefits

_____

_____

_____

DISPUTE AND RECONCILIATION
WORK SHEET

Group Members: _____   Date: _____

_____

_____

Use this work sheet to combine the information recorded on pages 59–61.

Problem:

_____

_____

Compromise:

_____

_____

Resolution:

_____

_____

Problem:

_____

_____

Compromise:

_____

_____

Resolution:

_____

_____

WIDGET COMPANY MANIFESTO WORK SHEET

Group Members: _____   Date: _____

_____

_____

This work sheet is the combination of the three separate work sheets created by workers, management, and the board of directors.

1. Mission Statement

_____

_____

_____

2. Company Philosophy

_____

_____

_____

3. Rules & Regulations

_____

_____

_____

4. Employee Benefits

_____

_____

_____

SEARCHING ON THE INTERNET

Directions: First, go to your favorite search engine or use one of the search engines listed below. Then use the keywords and phrases to locate Web sites for your project.

AltaVista	*http://www.altavista.com*
Excite	*http://www.excite.com*
Hotbot	*http://www.hotbot.com*
Lycos	*http://www.lycos.com*
Yahoo!	*http://www.yahoo.com*
Profusion	*http://www.profusion.com*

Keywords and Phrases

"Almanac of Birthdays"

"Bill of Rights"

Congress.gov

"Daily Almanac"

"Federal Constitution"

Fedworld

"Government Databases"

"House of Representatives"

"National Archives"

"Supreme Court"

"United Nations"

"US Congress"

"US Constitution"

"US Federal Agencies"

"US Institute of Peace" (USIP)

"US Senate"

"White House"

"World Government Documents"

PROGRAMS

- *If Monks Had Macs*—Voyager

- *Religions of the World*—Mentorom

- *World Beat*—Global Music

- *History and Culture of...*—Queue

- *Family Gathering*—Palladium

- *Family Tree Maker*—Broderbund

- *World Vista*—Applied Optical Media

- *US Government: First 200 Years*—Electronic Arts

- *Amnesty Interactive: Universal Declaration of Human Rights*—Amnesty International

- *Sim Tower*—Maxis

- *Zapatalism*—LavaMind

- *Ephemeral Films: 1931–1960*—Voyager

- *Our Secret Century*—Voyager

- *Makers of the 20th Century*—News Multimedia

- *Worlds' Greatest Speeches*—Softbit

THEME 6
POWER, AUTHORITY, AND GOVERNANCE

Social studies programs should include experiences that provide for the study of how people create and change structures of power, authority, and governance. Understanding the historical development of structures of power, authority, and governance and their evolving functions in contemporary United States society, as well as in other parts of the world, is essential for developing civic competence. In exploring this theme, students confront questions such as: What is power? What forms does it take? Who holds it? How is it gained, used, and justified? What is legitimate authority? How are governments created, structured, maintained, and changed? How can we keep government responsive to its citizens' needs and interests? How can individual rights be protected within the context of majority rule?

By examining the purposes and characteristics of various governance systems, learners develop an understanding of how groups and nations attempt to resolve conflicts and seek to establish order and security. Through study of the dynamic relationships among individual rights and responsibilities, the needs of social groups, and concepts of a just society, learners become more effective problem-solvers and decision-makers when addressing the persistent issues and social problems encountered in public life. They do so by applying concepts and methods of political science and law. In schools, this theme typically appears in units and courses dealing with government, politics, political science, history, law, and other social sciences.

Learners in the early grades explore their natural and developing sense of fairness and order as they experience relationships with others. They develop an increasingly comprehensive awareness of rights and responsibilities in specific contexts. During the middle school years, these rights and responsibilities are applied in more complex contexts with emphasis on new applications. High school students develop their abilities in the use of abstract principles. They study the various systems that have been developed over the centuries to allocate and employ power and authority in the governing process. At every level, learners should have opportunities to apply their knowledge and skills to and participate in the workings of the various levels of power, authority, and governance.

SCHOOL RULES

In the following set of lessons students will explore fairness and order as they experience relationships with others. As listed in the NCSS standards, "they develop an increasingly comprehensive awareness of rights and responsibilities in specific contexts." (This is your class' big chance!) In this first activity students generate a school from scratch and create a list of rules for their fantasy school.

Grade Level: three to five

Duration: one hour

Materials: Internet access

Procedure:

Before the Computer

- Begin a discussion about school rules and protocols.

  How are they formulated?
  Who decides?
  Can they be changed?

- Divide students into groups.
- Have each group generate a list of rules for a fantasy school.

On the Computer

- Research school rules from schools throughout history.
- What were the rules for the first public school in America? (Search hint: Boston)

After the Computer

- Compare the real school rules of your school to your fantasy school and to schools throughout history.
- Compare the different rules each group came up with.
- Discuss why or why not the fantasy school rules would be realistic.
- E-mail other schools around the country and gather lists of their rules.

FAIR OR UNFAIR

In this activity students hone their researching and reading skills on the Internet while developing an understanding of their moral beliefs and sense of fairness.

Grade Level: three to five

Duration: a week

Materials: Internet access, newspapers

Procedure:

Before the Computer

- Discuss a story in which an unfairness occurred.

- Over a period of a week have students review newspaper articles with their parents, looking for examples of unfairness.

- After students have collected their articles, chart the issues and categories on the board.

- From this list have students pick issues that concern them which they want to research in more depth.

On the Computer

- Have students search magazine and newspaper databases in search of articles relating to their "issue du jour."

- Select one article. Print it out. Outline its main points and give an oral presentation to the class.

- Examples of issues important to students include metal detectors in schools, forced dress codes, forced curfews, and corporal punishment.

Options:

- Rewrite an article from the opposing point of view.

- Do the same exercise using historical issues, articles, and reference material.

- Have students debate all sides of an issue, including the side they disagree with.

ALIEN TRAVEL, INC.

Students create travel brochures for extraterrestrials, describing Earth as either a fair or unfair planet.

Grade Level: three to five

Duration: three hours

Materials: copies of "Alien Brochure Work Sheet," page 70; word processing and desktop publishing software

Procedure:

Before the Computer

- Imagine that elementary school aliens from around the universe want to move to your town. To make their adjustment to earth easier, you have been selected to warn them of any inequalities and unfair practices that upper-elementary students face.

- Be sure your students understand issues of unfairness in your school and classroom.

- Discuss some unfair issues.

- Distribute the Alien Brochure Work Sheet. Review it to ensure your students have a firm grasp of the topic. (You may prefer to have students work in small groups.)

On the Computer

- Using a word processing software or desktop publishing program, design and create an alien brochure using interesting text and graphics.

- Print the brochures.

Option:

- Send the brochures to NASA via e-mail.

Earth is a fantastic place where the sky is actually blue. Don't expect to get your own way though. The teachers in school make you raise your tenticles before asking a question.

Come to Earth

TRAVEL

Visit

from **The PrintShop** from Broderbund

ALIEN BROCHURE WORK SHEET

Name(s): _____   Date: _____

The following are some helpful questions and suggestions to help you plan and design your brochure.

1. Possible unfair issues to discuss:

   bedtime

   homework

   curfew

   television

   school uniforms/dress codes

   grades

   daylight savings time

   standardized tests

2. Additional unfair issues:

   _____

   _____

   _____

3. Review some travel brochures for layout ideas.

4. Possible brochure layout:

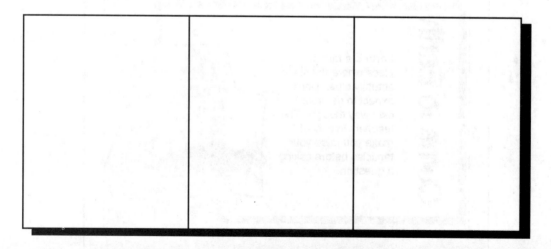

5. Design a rough sketch of your brochure on the back of this page.

UNIFORM FAIRNESS

Research schools that have uniform regulations and interview students.

Grade Level: three to five

Duration: two to four hours

Materials: word processing and database software, Internet access

Procedure:

Before the Computer

- Many schools require their students to wear uniforms. Create a questionnaire to send to schools in which students must wear uniforms. (The World Wide Web will be your best source of information for this.)

- Create a questionnaire to send to schools in which students don't wear uniforms.

- Design questions for comparative analysis. Some example questions follow:

    What's the grade point average of your school?

    Do you think people are happier or unhappier that they must wear uniforms?

    Do you feel a sense of belonging to your school?

    What's the point of school uniforms?

    Why are uniforms worn in the military?

    Why do airline pilots wear uniforms?

    Why do employees of fast food restaurants wear uniforms?

    Is a suit a uniform?

    What does the word "uniform" mean to you?

    What does the word "uniform" mean in your dictionary?

- Generate more questions on your own.

On the Computer

- Use database software to input all the information you've gathered from your questionnaire.

- Run correlations with your data. For example:

    Do students in schools that require uniforms have a higher GPA than students in school that don't?

- Print results and discuss.

Options:

- Create a newsletter (electronic and print) and write articles and pro/con editorials based on your results.

- Design your own uniform.

BRANCHES OF GOVERNMENT

Students will research the three branches of government using the Internet and other reference materials.

Grade Level: three to five

Duration: two hours

Materials: Internet access, CD-ROM encyclopedia

Procedure:

Before the Computer

- Divide your class into three groups.

- Assign each group to one of the three branches: judiciary, executive, and legislative.

- Prior to using the computer, discuss the structure of government and the membership and function of each group.

On the Computer

- Using the Internet and CD-ROM encyclopedias, have students research their branch of government.

- Have each group create multimedia, slide show, print, or video presentations about their branch of government and why they think their branch of government is the most important.

- Each group should discuss why or why not all three branches of government are necessary?

- Students should answer the following question:

  If you could restructure the government, what would you change?

Options:

- Videotape all three presentations to create a video of how the three branches relate. Share it with other classes.

- Do the same activity using other governments, such as the British or Israeli parliamentary system.

BILL OF RIGHTS MAKER

In this lesson students will study concepts of democracy as they create a classroom Bill of Rights.

Grade Level: three to five

Duration: 45 minutes

Materials: copies of "Bill of Rights Work Sheet," pages74–75; word processing and paint software; scanner; printer

Procedure:

Before the Computer

- Start with a group discussion of rights with the goal of defining what exactly a right is.
- Divide your class into small groups.
- Distribute the Bill of Rights Work Sheet.

On the Computer

- Using a word processing software and paint program, start from scratch and create a Bill of Rights.

After the Computer

- Compare the different sets of Bill of Rights.
- As a class, come up with a democratic method for combining all the groups' Bill of Rights.

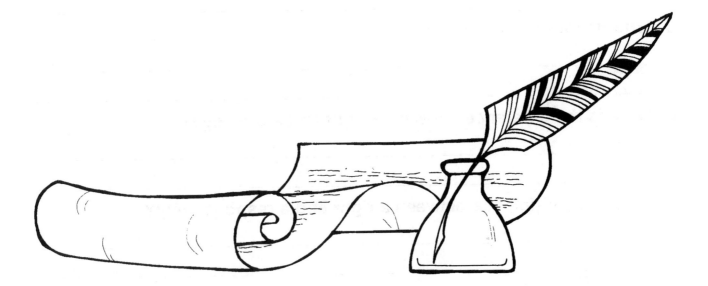

BILL OF RIGHTS WORK SHEET

Group Members: _____   Date: _____

_____

_____

Answer the following questions as you create your own definition for rights, responsibilites, and privilege.

1. What is a right?

_____

_____

2. What rights do students have?

_____

_____

3. What rights don't students have?

_____

_____

4. What rights do teachers have?

_____

_____

5. Who defines these rights?

_____

_____

6. What is the difference between a right and a privilege?

_____

_____

7. What's the difference between a right and a responsibility?

_____

_____

8. Is there such a thing as a universal right?

_____

_____

BILL OF RIGHTS WORK SHEET *(cont.)*

9. Research the Universal Bill of Human Rights.

_____

_____

_____

_____

10. Do two rights make a wrong?

_____

_____

_____

_____

11. Are there such things as birthrights?

_____

_____

_____

_____

12. What if someone's right infringes on yours?

_____

_____

_____

_____

TEN COMMANDMENTS

Comparing rights, privileges, obligations, and commandments, students further their thinking on structures of government and power as they develop their own "classroom commandments."

Grade Level: three to five

Duration: 45 minutes

Materials: copies of "Ten Commandments Work Sheet," page 77; word processing software; scanner

Procedure:

Before the Computer

- Compare the Ten Commandments to the Bill of Rights.
- Compare the Ten Commandments to our legal system.
- Discuss the idea behind the Ten Commandments.
- Break students up into groups.
- Pass out the work sheet, explaining that each group is to come up with a classroom commandment.

On the Computer

- Scan in the artwork.
- Shrink in *Photoshop,* if necessary.
- Have each group add their icon and commandment to a document, creating a list of classroom commandments.

Options:

- Have students work with their parents to come up with family commandments.
- Have students make personal commandments.

TEN COMMANDMENTS WORK SHEET

Group Members: _____   Date: _____

_____

_____

Our Commandment:

_____

_____

Reason for Our Commandment:

_____

_____

_____

Logo that Represents Our Commandment:

SEARCHING ON THE INTERNET

Directions: First, go to your favorite search engine or use one of the search engines listed below. Then use the keywords and phrases to locate Web sites for your project.

AltaVista	*http://www.altavista.com*
Excite	*http://www.excite.com*
Hotbot	*http://www.hotbot.com*
Lycos	*http://www.lycos.com*
Yahoo!	*http://www.yahoo.com*
Profusion	*http://www.profusion.com*

Keywords and Phrases

"Bill of Rights"

"Center for Civic Education"

"Civic Documents"

"Civic Network"

"Civic Practices"

"Civics Primer"

Congress.gov

Constitution

"Department of State"

"Federal Government Agencies"

"House of Representatives"

"Legislature"

"Library of Congress"

Senate

"Supreme Court"

"Supreme Court Cases"

"United Nations"

"US Capitol"

"US Congress"

"US Information Agency"

"White House"

"World Government Documents"

PROGRAMS

- *Time Multimedia Almanac*—Softkey

- *ABC Newslinks*—Creative Wonders

- *Encarta World Atlas*—Microsoft

- *In the First Degree*—Broderbund

- *US Government: The First 200 Years*—Electronic Arts

- *American History*—Clearvue

- *Amnesty Interactive: Universal Declaration of Human Rights*—Amnesty International

- *Origins of the Constitution*—Clearvue

- *Atlas Of US Presidents*—Applied Optical Media

- *Capitol Hill*—Mindscape

- *Doonesbury Election Game*—Mindscape

- *Decisions, Decisions: The Budget Process*—Tom Snyder Productions

- *Decisions, Decisions: Building a Nation*—Tom Snyder Productions

- *ABC NewsLinks: The Current Event Resource*—Creative Wonders

- *American Revolution*—Entrex

- *SimCity*—Maxis

- *A+LS Government*—American Education Corp.

- *Brown vs. Board of Education*—Guidance Associates

- *Congress: How a Bill Becomes a Law*—Guidance Associates

- *Choices, Choices: Taking Responsibility*—Tom Snyder Productions

- *Lest We Forget: Holocaust*—Research Systems

- *Makers of the 20th Century*—News Multimedia

THEME 7
PRODUCTION, DISTRIBUTION, AND CONSUMPTION

Social studies programs should include experiences that provide for the study of how people organize for the production, distribution, and consumption of goods and services. People have wants that often exceed the limited resources available to them. As a result, a variety of ways have been invented to decide upon answers to four fundamental questions: What is to be produced? How is production to be organized? How are goods and services to be distributed? What is the most effective allocation of the factors of production (land, labor, capital, and management)?

Unequal distribution of resources necessitates systems of exchange, including trade, to improve the well-being of the economy, while the role of government in economic policymaking varies over time and from place to place. Increasingly, these decisions are global in scope and require systematic study of an interdependent world economy and the role of technology in economic decision-making. In schools, this theme typically appears in units and courses dealing with concepts, principles, and issues drawn from the discipline of economics.

Young learners begin by differentiating between wants and needs. They explore economic decisions as they compare their own economic experiences with those of others and consider the wider consequences of those decisions on groups, communities, the nation, and beyond.

In the middle grades, learners expand their knowledge of economic concepts and principles and use economic reasoning processes in addressing issues related to the four fundamental economic questions.

High school students develop economic perspectives and deeper understanding of key economic concepts and processes through systematic study of a range of economic and sociopolitical systems, with particular emphasis on the examination of domestic and global economic policy options related to matters such as health care, resource use, unemployment, and trade.

COLLECTING LABELS

In this lesson students will collect labels and mark their geographic origin to show the widespread network of product production and consumption.

Grade Level: three to five

Duration: two days

Materials: butcher paper, mapping program, paint program, large map of the United States, scanner, *Photoshop*

Procedure:

Before the Computer

- Have students collect food labels that list origins for example, Washington apples, Idaho potatoes and Maine lobster.

On the Computer

- Using a scanner, scan in the labels. Using *Photoshop,* or another *Photoshop*-like program, reduce the labels to the size of a postage stamp. Print the labels on adhesive paper.

After the Computer

- Have students create a wall-sized map of the United States and attach the labels to their appropriate states.
- Discuss why products come from other states rather than being produced in your state.
- Discuss how these products got from their origin to your refrigerator or pantry.

Option:

- Use the classroom software program *National Inspirer* by Tom Snyder Productions.

PRODUCT TRAVEL LOG

In this lesson students will research and creatively describe the path a product must follow from inception to their kitchens.

Grade Level: three to five

Duration: 90 minutes

Materials: word processing software

Procedure:

Before the Computer

• Have students pick a product and research the process it went through to arrive in their kitchen.

On the Computer

• Have students write a day-by-day, first-person travel log and itinerary as if they were the product.

Here is an example of a day in the life of a Maine lobster.

Today was a really bad day. Not only did I swim right into a trap, but then I was plucked out of the water. What happened next was too much to bear. I was thrown into a huge vat of boiling water. Boy, did I see red!

After the Computer

• Read students' travel logs to the class.

Option:

• Perform the travel log as a play.

CREATE A PRODUCTION LINE

In this lesson students will simulate the assembly line process by creating and distributing a questionnaire throughout the school.

Grade Level: three to five

Duration: four hours

Materials: copies of "Efficacy Production Line Assessment Work Sheet," page 84; desktop publishing or word processing program, spreadsheet program

Procedure:

Before the Computer/On the Computer

- Divide the class into the following six groups:

    question generating group
    design layout group
    production group
    distribution group
    collection group
    analyze data group

- First, have the question generating group create the questions that will be used in the questionnaire. For example: What is your favorite breakfast cereal? Should all students be required to wear uniforms? Should art be mandatory in school?

- Next, have the design layout group create the format for the questionnaire and print it using *Page Maker* or other desktop publishing or word processing software.

After the Computer

- Have the production group copy, fold, and staple the questionnaires for distribution.

- The distribution group then plan distribution and collection of the questionnaire.

- The analysis group enters the results into a spreadsheet program

- Analyze the data to use for target marketing and focus groups for the following commercial activity.

Option:

- Distribute the Production Line Efficacy Assessment Work sheet. Fill it out and discuss the results and ways to improve the process. For example: What worked? What didn't work? Did you have fun? Does fun have to be a part of every activity?

EFFICACY PRODUCTION LINE ASSESSMENT WORK SHEET

Name: _____   **Date:** _____

1. **Did you think this was an efficient way to achieve our goals?**

   _____

   _____

   _____

2. **How was production line technology first used in this country?**

   _____

   _____

   _____

3. **What are the advantages of using a production line?**

   _____

   _____

   _____

4. **What are the disadvantages?**

   _____

   _____

   _____

5. **What other methods of production can you think of?**

   _____

MAKE AN ADVERTISEMENT

In this lesson students will create an advertisement and marketing plan to sell Swamp Slime, a product no one really wants.

Grade Level: three to five

Duration: two to four days

Materials: copies of "Swamp Slime Work Sheet," page 86; video camera and blank tape; desktop publishing program; slide show program; tape recorder and blank cassette

Procedure:

Before the Computer

- Break students up into four groups.
- Hand out the Swamp Slime Work Sheet.
- Go over the work sheet with the class.

On the Computer

- Have students produce their advertisements.

After the Computer

- Share the products with the class or other classes.

Swamp Slime

SWAMP SLIME WORK SHEET

Group Members: _____ Date: _____

_____

_____

"Swamp Slime" consists of a sealed yogurt sized container of green, mucky, swamp slime. Your job is to create an ad campaign to sell this new product. You may make a video, create a slide show, make a print ad, or create a radio advertisement. Your ad must convince people to buy this product.

Before you begin, consider the following:

What are possible uses for Swamp Slime?

_____

_____

_____

How will Swamp Slime improve the quality of peoples' lives? (squishing it is relaxing; coffee table item; can chase friends with it, etc.)

_____

_____

_____

Why can't people go without Swamp Slime? (relieves stress, everyone else has it, can dry it out and make things, etc.).

_____

_____

_____

Using the available tools, write your advertisement and produce it.

WANTS AND NEEDS

In this lesson students will learn and talk about the differences between wants and needs, the basic building blocks of our supply and demand economy.

Grade Level: three to five

Duration: 45 minutes

Materials: copies of "Desert Isle Work Sheet," page 88; word processing software; spreadsheet program; scanner; Internet access

Procedure:

Before the Computer

- Divide the class into five groups.
- Distribute the Desert Island Work sheet.
- Have each group select 10 items to bring to their desert island.
- When finished, have each group pass its work sheet to the group on the right.
- Explain to the class that due to Desert Isle baggage restrictions, each group can only bring five items.
- Have each group eliminate five of their neighboring group's items.
- Have each group explain why they crossed out each item.
- Use this as a seque into a discussion on the differences between wants and needs.
- Now have the class devise a method for reducing the number of items as a total class.
- Come up with definitions for the words want and need.

On the Computer

- Using word processing software, each group will create a wants/needs work sheet for the class.

After the Computer

- Share each group's list.

DESERT ISLE WORK SHEET

Group Members: _____   Date: _____

You find out you will be stranded on a desert island for one week. As a group, select 10 items to take along.

List of 10 things your group will take to the isle.

1. _____

2. _____

3. _____

4. _____

5. _____

6. _____

7. _____

8. _____

9. _____

10. _____

MINIMUM WAGE

In this lesson students will begin to learn about workers' rights, labor organizations, and economic reality by examining the history of the minimum wage.

Grade Level: three to five

Duration: two hours

Materials: Internet access, graphing program

Procedure:

Before the Computer

- Research the history of the minimum wage.

On the Computer

- Using *The Graph Club, ClarisWorks, GraphMaster,* or similar graphing program input your minimum wage data. Create and print graphs.
- Along with historical data research other countries' wage standards.

After the Computer

- Use this data to begin a discussion on minimum wage.
- Is there a maximum wage? Should there be?
- Why is there a minimum wage?
- How should minimum wage be set?
- Should American companies be allowed to have production sites in countries that don't have minimum wage standards?

Options:

- Research and track the cost of living during the same period.
- Create a cost of living graph.
- Are there any correlations between minimum wage and cost of living?
- Research some of the companies that have documented substandard working conditions and pay scale.

SEARCHING ON THE INTERNET

Directions: First, go to your favorite search engine or use one of the search engines listed below. Then use the keywords and phrases to locate Web sites for your project.

AltaVista	*http://www.altavista.com*
Excite	*http://www.excite.com*
Hotbot	*http://www.hotbot.com*
Lycos	*http://www.lycos.com*
Yahoo!	*http://www.yahoo.com*
Profusion	*http://www.profusion.com*

Keywords and Phrases

"50 States.com"

"American Memory"

"California Council for the Social Studies" (CCSS)

"Current Events" OR "Newspapers in Education"

"Global Environment"

"Green Peace"

"Interactive Atlas"

"K.I.D.S. Report Web Sites"

MapQuest

"National Council of Economic Education"

Thinkglobal

"World Bank"

"World Communities"

PROGRAMS

- *National Inspirer*—Tom Snyder Productions

- *International Inspirer*—Tom Snyder Productions

- *Oregon Trail*—MECC

- *SimCity*—Maxis

- *SimTower*—Maxis

- *Industrial Revolution in America*—Queue

- *TimeLiner*—Tom Snyder Productions

- *Strategy Games of the World*—Edmark

- *Physical World*—Mentorom

- *Small Blue Planet*—Cambrix

- *ABC NewsLinks*—Creative Wonders

- *The Face of Life*—Creative Multimedia

- *Critical Mass*—Corbis

- *Pony Express Rider*—McGraw Hill

- *Oregon Trail II*—MECC

- *Who Built America?*—Voyager

- *The Story of Civilization*—World Library

- *Explorers of the New World*—Future Vision

- *Chronicle of the 20th Century*—Dorling Kindersley

THEME 8
SCIENCE, TECHNOLOGY, AND SOCIETY

Social studies programs should include experiences that provide for the study of relationships among science, technology, and society. Technology is as old as the first crude tool invented by prehistoric humans, but today's technology forms the basis for some of our most difficult social choices.

Modern life as we know it would be impossible without technology and the science that supports it. But technology brings with it many questions: Is new technology always better than that which it will replace? What can we learn from the past about how new technologies result in broader social change, some of which is unanticipated? How can we cope with the ever-increasing pace of change, perhaps even with the feeling that technology has gotten out of control? How can we manage technology so that the greatest number of people benefit from it? How can we preserve our fundamental values and beliefs in a world that is rapidly becoming one technologically-linked village?

This theme appears in units or courses dealing with history, geography, economics, and civics and government. It draws upon several scholarly fields from the natural and physical sciences, social sciences, and the humanities for specific examples of issues and the knowledge base for considering responses to the societal issues related to science and technology.

Young children can learn how technologies form systems and how their daily lives are intertwined with a host of technologies. They can study how basic technologies such as ships, automobiles, and airplanes have evolved and how we have employed technology such as air conditioning, dams, and irrigation to modify our physical environment. From history (their own and others'), they can construct examples of how technologies such as the wheel, the stirrup, and the transistor radio altered the course of history.

By the middle grades, students can begin to explore the complex relationships among technology, human values, and behavior. They will find that science and technology bring changes that surprise us and even challenge our beliefs, as in the case of discoveries and their applications related to our universe, the genetic basis of life, atomic physics, and others.

As they move from the middle grades to high school, students will need to think more deeply about how we can manage technology so that we control it rather than the other way around. There should be opportunities to confront such issues as the consequences of using robots to produce goods, the protection of privacy in the age of computers and electronic surveillance, and the opportunities and challenges of genetic engineering, test-tube life, and medical technology with all their implications for longevity and quality of life and religious beliefs.

CARTOON TOOLS

In this activity students will use technology to define technology.

Grade Level: three to five

Duration: six hours

Materials: copies of "Define a Tool Work Sheet," page 94; presentation program

Procedure:

Before the Computer

- Divide the class into pairs.
- Have each group pick a simple tool with no moving parts, such as a wheel, hammer, knife, fork, pliers, or ice-cream scoop.
- Have students create a cartoon character that is a personification of their chosen tool.
- Have students make a storyboard for a cartoon that explains why that tool is important and what the world would be like if it hadn't been developed.

On the Computer

- Have students create an animated movie, slideshow, or presentation of their cartoon using a program such as *ClarisWorks Slideshow, Kid Pix Slideshow, Hyperstudio, Director,* or *Aldus Premier.*
- Remind students that the sophistication of their animated presentation is not important. Stick figures are fine.

After the Computer

- Distribute the Define a Tool Work sheet.

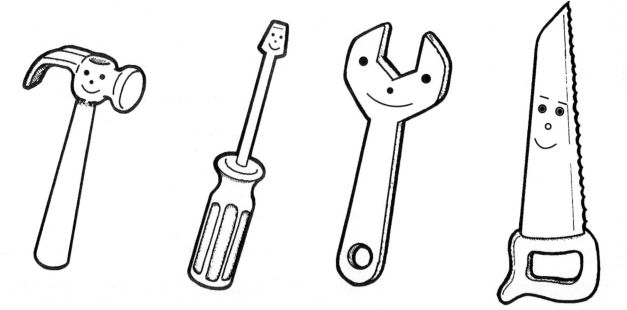

DEFINE A TOOL WORK SHEET

Group Members: _____   Date: _____

_____

_____

1. What are some of the common elements of the tools in your presentation?

_____

_____

_____

2. What was the first tool?

_____

_____

_____

3. What do tools help us do?

_____

_____

_____

4. List the tools that you use on a regular basis.

_____

_____

_____

5. Is television a tool?

_____

_____

_____

DEFINE A TOOL WORK SHEET *(cont.)*

6. Are all tools good?

_____

_____

_____

7. Do only humans use tools?

_____

_____

_____

8. What are some tools you would like to invent?

_____

_____

_____

9. What tools do you have access to that your parents didn't?

_____

_____

_____

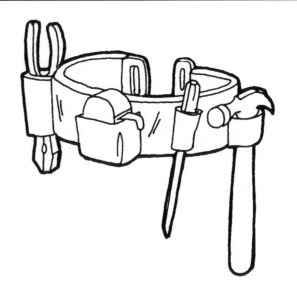

REINVENTING THE WHEEL— THE PROBLEMS WITH TECHNOLOGY

Typically, we think of technology as something positive. In this lesson students will examine some of the negative effects of technological advances throughout time.

Grade Level: three to five

Duration: 45 minutes

Materials: copies of "Plusses of Technology Work Sheet," page 97, and "Minuses of Technology Work sheet," page 98; CD-ROM encyclopedia; Internet access

Procedure:

Before the Computer

- You will be dividing your class into groups that will debate the pros and cons of different modes of transportation. We have selected five modes of transportation. Assign two groups—one pro, one con—to each mode of transport. Feel free to use other appropriate transportation technology.

- Divide the class into 10 groups.

- Distribute the Plusses of Technology Work Sheet to half of the groups.

- Distribute the Minuses of Technology Work Sheet to the other half.

- Assign one of the following technologies to each of the groups:

  > *train*
  >
  > *skateboard*
  >
  > *airplane*
  >
  > *ship*
  >
  > *automobile*

- Groups must create a presentation defending or opposing their technology.

On the Computer

- Use the Internet and CD-ROM for research.

Option:

- Try this same activity with other technologies students choose to explore.

PLUSSES OF TECHNOLOGY WORK SHEET

Group Members: _____   Date: _____

_____

_____

1. Our group's mode of transport is _____.

2. What problems did the invention of this technology solve?

   _____

   _____

3. How has this invention improved peoples' lives?

   _____

   _____

4. What are some creative uses of this particular transportation?

   _____

   _____

5. What problems would occur if this transportation suddenly became unavailable?

   _____

   _____

6. Why is this mode of transportation better than others?

   _____

   _____

7. What jobs were created because of this transportation?

   _____

   _____

MINUSES OF TECHNOLOGY WORK SHEET

Group Members: _____   Date: _____

_____

_____

1. Our group's mode of transportation is _____.

2. What problems did the invention of this technology cause?

   _____

   _____

3. How has this invention hindered peoples' lives?

   _____

   _____

4. What are some problematic uses of this particular transportation?

   _____

   _____

5. What problems would be solved if this transportation suddenly became unavailable?

   _____

   _____

6. Why is this mode of transportation worse than others?

   _____

   _____

7. What jobs were lost because of this transportation?

   _____

   _____

SCIENCE APPLY-ENCE

Your class takes on the role of a group of historical scientists who need funding for their projects. Each group must create a persuasive presentation arguing for funding.

Grade Level: three to five

Duration: three hours

Materials: copies of "Science Apply-ence Funding Work Sheet," page 100; Internet access; CD-ROM encyclopedia; multimedia presentation software

Procedure:

Before the Computer

- Divide your class into groups of four.

- Have each group pick a scientific invention or technology from history and argue why it should be funded. Explain to the class that there is only enough funding for two of these historical inventions. (Examples include telephone, electricity, space exploration, printing press, polio vaccine, nuclear weapons, and guns.)

On the Computer

- Use the Internet, CD-ROM encyclopedia, and other sources for research

- Create a presentation, using *KidPix 2* or *ClarisWorks,* to persuade the class your scientific invention is necessary over all the others.

After the Computer

- Have students make their presentations.

- Have groups vote on which two projects get funded.

Thomas Edison

SCIENCE APPLY-ENCE FUNDING WORK SHEET

Group Members: _____   Date: _____

_____

_____

1. Scientific Invention or Technology

   _____

   _____

2. Benefits and Potential Benefits

   _____

   _____

3. What problems would our society have faced if this item had not invented?

   _____

   _____

4. Possible pitfalls of invention and ways to mitigate them

   _____

   _____

5. Why we alone should get the money

   _____

   _____

BLINDED BY SCIENCE

Students create comparative time lines of history and technology and explore the impact one has on the other.

Grade Level: three to five

Duration: two hours

Materials: copies of "Blinded by Science Work Sheet," page 102; time line program (if available)

Procedure:

Before the Computer

- Have each student create two separate time lines—one including key historical events, the other including key scientific inventions from 1900 to the present.

- Have each student pick one scientific invention and pretend that it was never invented.

- Now have students create a third time line showing how the events in history would have been changed without the invention of this technology. Students should change, delete, and add historical events as they rewrite history.

On the Computer

- Create the time line using a paint program or *TimeLiner* by Tom Snyder Productions.

After the Computer

- Redo this activity using present technologies and future time lines.

BLINDED BY SCIENCE WORK SHEET

Name: _____   Date: _____

1. Key historical events from 1900 to the present:

   _____

   _____

   _____

2. Key technological events from 1900 to the present:

   _____

   _____

   _____

3. Technology you choose to eliminate:

   _____

   _____

   _____

4. Events that occurred because of this technology:

   _____

   _____

   _____

5. How certain events would have been changed if this technology had not been invented:

   _____

   _____

   _____

6. Make up pretend events that occurred because this technology was not invented:

   _____

   _____

   _____

SEARCHING ON THE INTERNET

Directions: First, go to your favorite search engine or use one of the search engines listed below. Then use the keywords and phrases to locate Web sites for your project.

AltaVista	*http://www.altavista.com*
Excite	*http://www.excite.com*
Hotbot	*http://www.hotbot.com*
Lycos	*http://www.lycos.com*
Yahoo!	*http://www.yahoo.com*
Profusion	*http://www.profusion.com*

Keywords and Phrases

"A-Bomb Museum"

CIA

"Classroom Connect"

"Daily Almanac"

Discovery.com

"Electronic Journal"

Enlightenment

"Global Environment"

IBM

JPL

"K.I.D.S. Report Web Sites"

"Museum Hotlist"

"National Archives"

PBS

Renaissance

"United Nations"

PROGRAMS

- *The Way Things Work*—Dorling Kindersley
- *If Monks Had Macs: Arts & Ideas*—Voyager
- *SimCity*—Maxis
- *SimTown*—Maxis
- *SimTower*—Maxis
- *Encarta World Atlas*—Microsoft
- *Time Multimedia Almanac*—Softkey
- *Encarta World Atlas*—Microsoft
- *Critical Mass: The Race to Build the Atomic Bomb*—Corbis
- *The Story of Civilization*—World Library
- *Flagtower 20th Century: Primary Source Documents*—Flagtower
- *Exploring Ancient Cities*—Sumeria
- *Leonardo the Inventer*—Interactive Electronic Pub
- *Explorers of The New World*—Future Vision
- *How Would You Survive?*—Grolier
- *History Of The World*—Dorling Kindersley
- *Chronicle Of The 20th Century*—Dorling Kindersley
- *The Clothes We Wore*—E.M.M.E.
- *Mythology*—Thomas S. Klise
- *Origins of Mankind: 70 Million Years of Content*—Maris
- *TimeLiner*—Tom Snyder Productions
- *The Makers of the 20th Century*—News Multimedia
- *Science Court—Work and Simple Machines*—Tom Snyder Productions

THEME 9
GLOBAL CONNECTIONS

Social studies programs should include experiences that provide for the study of global connections and interdependence. The realities of global interdependence require understanding the increasingly important and diverse global connections among world societies. Analysis of tensions between national interests and global priorities contributes to the development of possible solutions to persistent and emerging global issues in many fields: health care, economic development, environmental quality, universal human rights, and others.

Analyzing patterns and relationships within and among world cultures, such as economic competition and interdependence, age-old ethnic enmities, political and military alliances, and others, helps learners carefully examine policy alternatives that have both national and global implications. This theme typically appears in units or courses dealing with geography, culture, and economics but again can draw upon the natural and physical sciences and the humanities, including literature, the arts, and language. Through exposure to various media and firsthand experiences, young learners become aware of and are affected by events on a global scale.

Within this context, students in early grades examine and explore global connections and basic issues and concerns, suggesting and initiating responsive action plans. In the middle years, learners can initiate analysis of the interactions among states and nations and their cultural complexities as they respond to global events and changes. At the high school level, students are able to think systematically about personal, national, and global decisions, interactions, and consequences, including addressing critical issues such as peace, human rights, trade, and global ecology.

UNITED NATIONS TRADING CARDS

In this exercise students will research the origin of the United Nations by creating trading cards with statistical information about member countries and their leaders.

Grade Level: three to five

Duration: two to four hours

Materials: copies of "UN Trading Card Work Sheet," page 107; Internet access; CD-ROM encyclopedia; database software

Procedure:

Before the Computer

- Distribute copies of the UN Trading Card Work Sheet to students.
- Use whatever method you prefer to divide the UN member countries among your students.

On the Computer

- Each student will use CD-ROM encyclopedias, the World Wide Web, and other reference materials to complete five trading cards.

Options:

- Scan cards into the computer, colorize then in a paint program, print them onto cardstock or adhesive paper to create UN stickers.
- Collect them, trade them, and save them!

UNITED NATIONS TRADING CARDS WORKSHEET

Group Members: _____   Date: _____
_____
_____

Nation _____
UN member since _____
Head of Grovement _____
Population _____
Language _____
GNP _____
Highest elevation _____
Lowest elevation _____
Draw the country's flag.

Additional interesting facts about this country:
_____
_____
_____

© *Teacher Created Materials, Inc.*   107   *#2431 Integrating Technology—Social Studies*

UNITED NATIONS TRADING CARDS WORK SHEET

Group Members: _____   Date: _____

_____

_____

Nation _____

UN member since _____

Head of Grovernment _____

Population _____

Language _____

GNP _____

Highest elevation_____

Lowest elevation _____

Draw the country's flag.

Additional interesting facts about this country:

_____

_____

_____

_____

E-MAIL THE WORLD

In this exercise students will reach out to the four corners of the globe contacting and exchanging letters with people from other countries. Students will compete with each other to receive the most e-mail from different countries around the world.

Grade Level: three to five

Duration: ongoing

Materials: Internet access, student e-mail journals

Procedure:

Before the Computer

- Explain to students that they will be forming e-mail pen pals around the world and they will need a place to keep and display all the replies they receive.

- Have students design and create their own e–mail journals in which they can paste all the e-mails they receive. They can make their journals or use premade ones.

- Students can decorate the pages with appropriate icons from each country, such as flags or other symbols.

On the Computer

- Surf the Internet to find students or other people you can e-mail with the hope of getting a response.

- A good way to find addresses is to use key words to get to individual, corporate, or educational Web sites from other countries. Many of these sites will have an e-mail button or specific addresses to which one can write.

- Encourage students to explore as many countries as they can.

Options:

- Create a wall-sized world map and have students pin their e-mails on the appropriate country.

- Collect a word in the language of each country. See which person gets the most translations for a word like "hello."

WORLD-WIDE WORD SEARCH

Students use a spreadsheet program to create a word search puzzle using the names of all the countries in the world. This lesson can be used on its on or in combination with the previous E-mail the World exercise.

Grade Level: three to five

Duration: two to three hours

Materials: spreadsheet program, mapping program

Procedure:

Before the Computer

- Generate a list of the different countries in the world. Divide this list among students.
- Have each students create a print version of their puzzle.

On the Computer

- Enter the puzzle into a spreadsheet.

Options:

- Challenge students to create a puzzle directly on the spreadsheet without a print version.
- Print a wall-sized copy of your puzzle.
- Create continent-based puzzles.
- Create a puzzle using capital cities.

```
G  B  L  A  D  Y  B  I  R  D
M  E  P  O  S  P  O  T  S  B
T  L  C  L  A  R  V  A  S  E
H  Y  A  P  H  I  D  M  C  E
O  T  P  H  O  E  S  C  A  T
R  R  E  M  P  U  P  A  L  L
A  A  S  O  E  G  G  S  E  E
X  Y  T  L  B  W  I  N  G  S
W  L  S  T  I  N  S  E  C  T
```

ADDRESSING THE GLOBE

In this lesson students will hone their research skills while continuing to build their knowledge base of the countries of the world.

Grade Level: three to five

Duration: one hour

Materials: copies of "Addressing the Globe Work Sheet," page 111; Internet access

Procedure:

Before the Computer

- Copy and distribute the Addressing the Globe work sheet.
- Have students pick five countries in which they are interested.

On the Computer

- Using a search engine such as *Yahoo!com*, *Excite.com*, or *Lycos.com*, have students perform a search on the countries of interest.
- Have students compile a list of fun, useful URLs related to their chosen countries with descriptions of the sites.

Options:

- Compile all the information into a World URL Journal for reference. Share with other classes.
- Create a scavenger hunt for other students, using your URLs.

ADDRESSING THE GLOBE WORK SHEET

Name _____   Date: _____

| | **Country of Choice** | **Interesting URL** |

1.

_____   _____

Comments and Rating of This URL

_____

_____

_____

2.

_____   _____

Comments and Rating of This URL

_____

_____

_____

3.

_____   _____

Comments and Rating of This URL

_____

_____

_____

4.

_____   _____

Comments and Rating of This URL

_____

_____

_____

SEARCHING ON THE INTERNET

Directions: First, go to your favorite search engine or use one of the search engines listed below. Then use the keywords and phrases to locate Web sites for your project.

AltaVista	*http://www.altavista.com*
Excite	*http://www.excite.com*
Hotbot	*http://www.hotbot.com*
Lycos	*http://www.lycos.com*
Yahoo!	*http://www.yahoo.com*
Profusion	*http://www.profusion.com*

Keywords and Phrases

"A-Bomb Museum"
"Amnesty International"
Artists (Try the Yahoo subject lists to retrieve a long list of artists)
CNN
Discovery.com
"Diverse Cultures"
Diversity
"Earth Images"
"Ellis Island"
Enlightenment
"Gateway to World History"
"Global Environment"
"Global Study Guides"
Hyperhistory
"Interactive Maps"
MapQuest
"Museum Hotlist"
NCSS
"Newspapers in Education"
Renaissance
Thinkglobal
"World Communities"
"World War II"

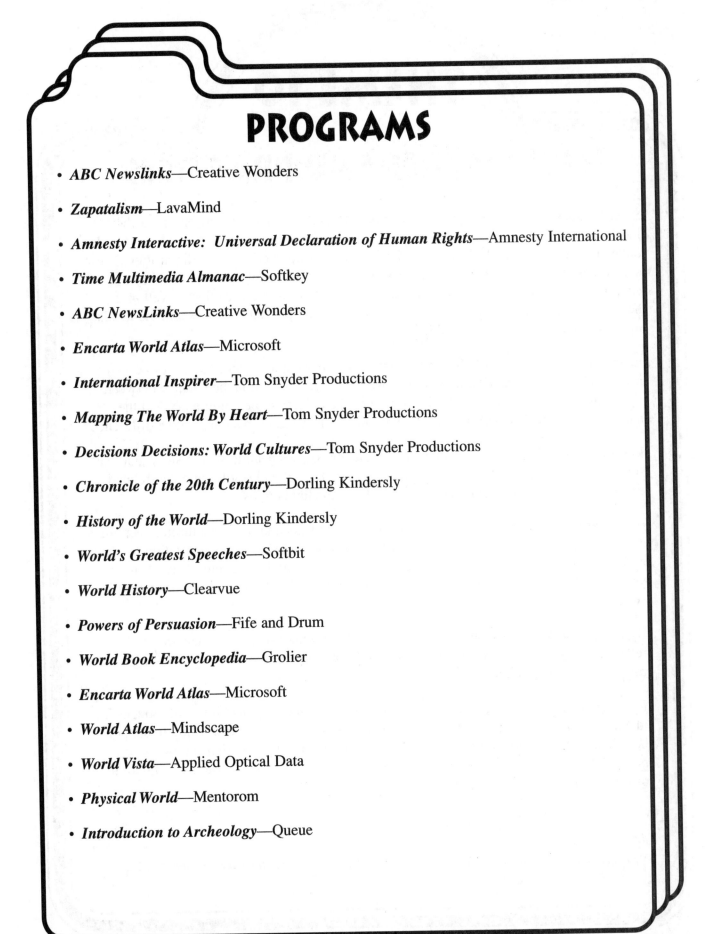

PROGRAMS

- *ABC Newslinks*—Creative Wonders

- *Zapatalism*—LavaMind

- *Amnesty Interactive: Universal Declaration of Human Rights*—Amnesty International

- *Time Multimedia Almanac*—Softkey

- *ABC NewsLinks*—Creative Wonders

- *Encarta World Atlas*—Microsoft

- *International Inspirer*—Tom Snyder Productions

- *Mapping The World By Heart*—Tom Snyder Productions

- *Decisions Decisions: World Cultures*—Tom Snyder Productions

- *Chronicle of the 20th Century*—Dorling Kindersly

- *History of the World*—Dorling Kindersly

- *World's Greatest Speeches*—Softbit

- *World History*—Clearvue

- *Powers of Persuasion*—Fife and Drum

- *World Book Encyclopedia*—Grolier

- *Encarta World Atlas*—Microsoft

- *World Atlas*—Mindscape

- *World Vista*—Applied Optical Data

- *Physical World*—Mentorom

- *Introduction to Archeology*—Queue

THEME 10
CIVIC IDEALS AND PRACTICES

Social studies programs should include experiences that provide for the study of the ideals, principles, and practices of citizenship in a democratic republic. An understanding of civic ideals and practices of citizenship is critical to full participation in society and is a central purpose of the social studies. All people have a stake in examining civic ideals and practices across time and in diverse societies as well as at home and in determining how to close the gap between present practices and the ideals upon which our democratic republic is based.

Learners confront such questions as: What is civic participation and how can I be involved? How has the meaning of citizenship evolved? What is the balance between rights and responsibilities? What is the role of the citizen in the community and the nation and as a member of the world community? How can I make a positive difference?

In schools, this theme typically appears in units or courses dealing with history, political science, and cultural anthropology and in fields such as global studies and law-related education, while also drawing upon content from the humanities.

In the early grades, students are introduced to civic ideals and practices through activities such as helping to set classroom expectations, examining experiences in relation to ideals, and determining how to balance the needs of individuals and the group. During these years, children also experience views of citizenship in other times and places through stories and drama.

By the middle grades, students expand their ability to analyze and evaluate the relationships between ideals and practices. They are able to see themselves taking civic roles in their communities.

High school students increasingly recognize the rights and responsibilities of citizens in identifying societal needs, setting directions for public policies, and working to support both individual dignity and the common good. They learn by experience how to participate in community service and political activities and how to use the democratic process to influence public policy.

PAPER TRAIL

Students will take the freedom of speech ideal from abstract to concrete by creating a classroom paper or newsletter.

Grade Level: three to five

Duration: ongoing

Materials: word processing or desktop publishing software

Procedure:

Before the Computer

- This is a very comprehensive activity that should be ongoing. Creating a newspaper provides a lot of opportunities for students to voice their opinions, share important and interesting ideas and facts, and to have a regular forum for discussion.

- Divide the class into groups of four.

- Have each group select a topic that directly or indirectly involves the school or local community and relates to civic ideals and practices.

- Have each group research and write their articles in newspaper style.

On the Computer

- Design and create the newspapers.

- Some good programs to use for desktop publishing include any word processing software or layout programs such as *QuarkXPress* or *PageMaker*.

- Often it is easy to create a layout template that can be used each week so students can focus on their writing.

After the Computer

- Print and distribute the classroom paper.

Options:

- Create an online Internet paper.

- Add a weekly advice column that other students in the school can respond to.

SCHOOLOCRACY

Students will directly experience civic ideals and practices by creating and developing a mock school. In this exciting roleplaying activity, students experience the intricate machinations involved in running a public organization. This lesson plan can be used in conjunction with the Widget World, Inc. activity on page 58 which focuses on similar issues within a private corporation.

Grade Level: three to five

Duration: ongoing

Materials: copies of "Schoolocracy Work Sheet," page 117; paint program

Procedure:

Before the Computer

- Divide the class into three groups: teachers, students, and administrators.

- Have each group fill out their personal Schoolocracy Work Sheet completing it from their assigned perspective.

- Explain to students that different groups within the same structure often have contrasting, conflicting, or opposing points of view. The goal of this activity is to work with these different ideals to create a unified organization.

On the Computer

- Have each of the three groups use the computer to design their school from the perspective of the group they represent. For example, teachers would want a bigger teachers' lounge, more time for preparation, students might want a bigger playground, less homework, more meaningful activities, and administrators might want more rules and regulations.

- Use a word processing software to put together your comprehensive school proposal package.

After the Computer

- After each group completes their work sheet, they must come together as a company and complete the final work sheet.

Option:

- Create a multimedia presentation of your school design and proposal.

SCHOOLOCRACY WORK SHEET: TEACHERS

Name: _____   Date: _____

Complete the work sheet from your perspective as a teacher.

1. School Mission Statement

_____

_____

_____

_____

2. School Philosophy

_____

_____

_____

_____

3. Rules & Regulations

_____

_____

_____

_____

4. Schedule

_____

_____

_____

_____

SCHOOLOCRACY WORK SHEET: STUDENTS

Name: _____   Date: _____

Complete the work sheet from your perspective as a student.

1. School Mission Statement

   _____
   _____
   _____
   _____

2. School Philosophy

   _____
   _____
   _____
   _____

3. Rules & Regulations

   _____
   _____
   _____
   _____

4. Schedule

   _____
   _____
   _____
   _____

SCHOOLOCRACY WORK SHEET: ADMINISTRATORS

Name: _____ Date: _____

Complete the work sheet from your perspective as an administrator.

1. School Mission Statement

   _____

   _____

   _____

   _____

2. School Philosophy

   _____

   _____

   _____

   _____

3. Rules & Regulations

   _____

   _____

   _____

   _____

4. Schedule

   _____

   _____

   _____

   _____

CITIZENS OF THE WORLD IN SCHOOL

In the following three progressive lessons students will identify what it means to be a "good" citizen—beginning with school citizenship, leading to American citizenship, and finishing with global citizenship.

Grade Level: three to five

Duration: four to six hours

Materials: Internet access, database and graphing program, CD-ROM encyclopedia

Procedure:

Before the Computer

- Discuss as a class what it means to belong to a school community. What are some of the rights, responsibilities, and privileges? Use the results from the previous Schoolocracy activity to promote discussion.

- From this discussion generate a list of quantifiable "good" student characteristics and behaviors. Some examples might be raising your hand to speak, remaining quiet, listening to your teacher, showing up on time, etc. Discuss with your students who decides whether these characteristics are important.

- As a class, prioritize the list of characteristics.

- Create a survey for other classes in the school asking them to prioritize the characteristics you generated.

On the Computer

- Have students enter the information from their school survey into a database and a graphing program.

- Publish the results in a newsletter your class designs using a desktop publisher.

- Distribute the newsletter to the school.

Option:

- Create an electronic version of your newsletter and e-mail it to your schoolmates and around the world.

CITIZENS OF THE WORLD IN AMERICA

Students will continue their exploration of the meaning of "good" citizenship, widening their perspective to the national level.

Grade Level: three to five

Duration: two hours

Materials: CD-ROM, Internet access, desktop publishing program

Procedure:

Before the Computer

- Use the Internet to research original source material on citizenship from the time of the Founding Fathers to the present.

- Based on the research, generate your own Bill of Rights for American citizens.

- What characteristics are different between school citizenship and national citizenship?

On the Computer

- Use a desktop publishing program to create and publish a new founding fathers' and founding mothers' Bill of Rights.

Options:

- Take your new Bill of Rights home and discuss with your family. Would they agree with it?

- Compare the American Bill of Rights with another country's equivalent of the Bill of Rights.

- What might have been different in our original Bill of Rights if women's perspectives had been included along with those of the founding fathers?

- Support continuing discussions on what it means to be an American.

CITIZENS OF THE WORLD IN THE WORLD

Students continue their exploration of the meaning of "good" citizenship, widening their perspective to the global level.

Grade Level: three to five

Duration: two to four hours

Materials: copies of "World Citizens Work sheet," page 123; Internet access; CD-ROM encyclopedia

Procedure:

Before the Computer

- Now that your students have an understanding of human rights and citizenship at the local and national levels, they can apply what they've learned to the "Global Village."

- Distribute the World Citizens Work sheet.

On the Computer

- Find Internet sites of international human rights organizations such as Greenpeace, Amnesty International, Peace Corps, and others.

- Most likely these sites will have the information students need to complete their work sheets.

- Input information into a relational database.

After the Computer

- Compare these different organizations and their basic tenets.

- Present the completed work sheets to the entire class.

- Have students create their own human rights organization with a global Bill of Rights.

Options:

- Create a Web page for the new organizations.

- Create a fund-raiser to raise funds and support for a global organization of choice.

- Discuss the differences, possible conflicts, and interelatedness among American citizenship, community citizenship, and world citizenship.

WORLD CITIZENS WORK SHEET

Name: _____   Date: _____

Use this work sheet to compile data on various global civic organizations.

Name of Organization_____

Date of Inception_____

Mission Statement _____

_____

_____

_____

_____

_____

Organization's Current Projects

_____

_____

_____

_____

Why is this organization important?

_____

_____

_____

How does this organization support the concepts of citizenship earlier discussed?

_____

_____

_____

CIVIC CURRENCY

In this activity students will get a chance to commemorate their favorite civic leaders and celebrate their achievements by redesigning United States currency using civic leaders of their choice.

Grade Level: three to five

Duration: two hours

Materials: copies of "Civic Currency Template, page 125; *Photoshop* or equivalent paint program; scanner

Procedure:

Before the Computer

- Divide the class into development teams of three or four members
- Pass out the Civic Currency Template to guide students in their designs.
- Each team must redesign from scratch United States currency, deciding on denominations, design, person honored, and reason why that person was chosen.
- Add relevant characteristics, issues, icons, and symbols to your currency. For example, students can choose to create a ten dollar bill with Maya Angelou as the person honored. Students may choose to incorporate excerpts from her poetry and images from her life experiences in the design.

On the Computer

- Using *Photoshop*, or an equivalent program, design your currency.

After the Computer

- Print currencies.

Options:

- Create postage stamps.
- Create currency for other countries.
- Create an intra-classroom economy based on the new currency in which the students' money has "value."

CIVIC CURRENCY TEMPLATE

Name: _____   Date: _____

Use these questions to help you design your currency.

1. What is this person's greatest accomplishment?

   _____

   _____

2. Can this accomplishment be conveyed in a picture or drawing?

   _____

   _____

3. What important details must be on your currency?

   _____

   _____

4. What symbols best represent your chosen civic leader's ideals?

   _____

   _____

5. What colors are appropriate for your currency?

   _____

   _____

6. What words, quotes, sayings should be on your currency?

   _____

   _____

7. What animal, place, or thing might be appropriate for your currency?

   _____

   _____

8. What will you call your currency (e.g. dollar, pound, cruzeiro, franc, pesos etc.)?

   _____

   _____

VIDEO RIGHTS

Students will create a two minute video public service announcement (PSA) about a great civic and human rights leader from any period in history.

Grade Level: three to five

Duration: six to eight hours

Materials: copies of "Civic Leader Video Work sheets I & II," pages 127–128; VCR; CD-ROM encyclopedia; Internet access; multimedia presentation program

Procedure:

Before the VCR:

- Explain to students how PSAs have been historically used to promote various causes and ideals. Because of the brevity of the announcement this format forces students to focus on the key points and incorporate them quickly and efficiently into a cohesive and persuasive presentation.

- Have students pick a civic leader from the Civic Leader Video Work sheet I, or select one of their own.

- Divide students into groups based on their favorite civic leaders.

- Use the Internet and other reference materials to research these leaders.

On the VCR

- Produce a video interview, PSA, or other type of presentation.

After the VCR

- Share with the class.

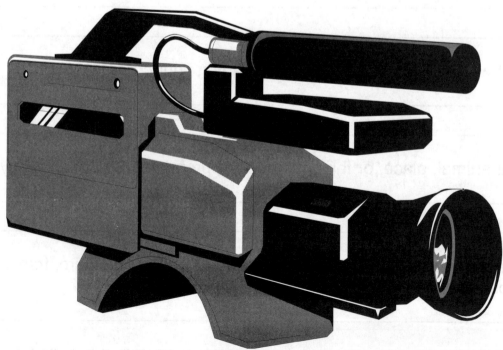

CIVIC LEADER VIDEO WORK SHEET I

- Martin Luther King, Jr.

- Harriet Tubman

- Malcolm X

- Susan B. Anthony

- John F. Kennedy

- Mahatma Ghandi

- Nelson Mandela

- Shirley Chisholm

- Cesar Chavez

- Sojourner Truth

- George Bush

- Abraham Lincoln

- Rosa Parks

- Thomas Jefferson

- Princess Diana

- Jimmy Carter

- Bishop Desmond Tutu

- Mother Theresa

- Elizabeth Stanton

- Anwar Sadat

- Harriet Beecher Stowe

- General Colin Powell

CIVIC LEADER VIDEO WORK SHEET II

Name: _____   Date: _____

Use this work sheet to help you create your video or multimedia presentation.

Name of civic leader _____

Birthplace _____

Birth/Death dates _____

Accomplishments _____

_____

_____

_____

_____

_____

_____

_____

Important points to make in video

1. _____

_____

_____

2. _____

_____

_____

3. _____

_____

_____

SEARCHING ON THE INTERNET

Directions: First, go to your favorite search engine or use one of the search engines listed below. Then use the keywords and phrases to locate Web sites for your project.

AltaVista	*http://www.altavista.com*
Excite	*http://www.excite.com*
Hotbot	*http://www.hotbot.com*
Lycos	*http://www.lycos.com*
Yahoo!	*http://www.yahoo.com*
Profusion	*http://www.profusion.com*

Keywords and Phrases

"Bill of Rights"

"Center for Civic Education"

"Civic Documents"

"Civic Network"

"Civic Practices"

"Civics Primer"

Congress.gov

Constitution

"Department of State"

"Federal Government Agencies"

"House of Representatives"

"Legislature"

"Library of Congress"

Senate

"Supreme Court"

"Supreme Court Cases"

"United Nations"

"US Capitol"

"US Congress"

"US Information Agency"

"White House"

"World Government Documents"

PROGRAMS

- *The Face Of Life*—Creative Multimedia
- *African-American: Slavery To Civil Rights*—Queue
- *Powers Of Persuasion*—Fife and Drum
- *American Indian Encyclopedia*—Facts on File
- *Landmark Documents In American History*—Facts on File
- *A House Divided*—CGRafica Multimedia
- *CD Source Book Of American History*—Compact University
- *Critical Mass*—Corbis
- *Reel Women*—Enteractive
- *Pony Express Rider*—Mcgraw-Hill
- *Oregon Trail II*—MECC
- *The Crucible*—Penguin —Witches And Such
- *Malcolm X: By Any Means Necessary*—Scholastic
- *Selected Civil War Photographs*—Stokes Imaging Services
- *The War In Vietnam*—Digital USA
- *150 Years Of Americas*—Macmillan Digital USA
- *Lincoln*—Sunburst
- *Who Built America: Immigration 1876–1914*—Voyager
- *Ephemeral Films: 1931–1960*—Voyager
- *Our Secret Century: Darker Side of Our Collective Past*—Voyager
- *Her Heritage: Famous American Women*—Pilgrim New Media

World History

- *WWII Global Conflict*—Mentorom
- *The Silk Road: China*—DNA Multimedia
- *World History*—Clearvue
- *The Story of Civilization: From 40,000 BC Through the French Revolution*—World Library
- *Flagtower 20th Century*—Flagtower
- *Origins of Mankind: 70 million Years of Content*—Maris
- *Lest We Forget: Holocaust*—Research Systems
- *Makers of the 20th Century*—News Multimedia
- *World's Greatest Speeches*—Softbit
- *Microsoft Bookshelf*—Encarta
- *World Book Encyclopedia*—Grolier
- *Bartlett's Familiar Quotations*—Time Warner

130

BRAINSTORMING WORDS

This brainstorming page is a separate general reference page that can be used to spark thoughts and ideas for many of the lessons and discussions. Generate more brainstorming words with your students to add to the list.

- History
- Innocent
- Torture
- Subjugation
- Freedom
- Equality
- Indigenous
- Sacrifice
- Intelligence
- Authoritarian
- Content
- Drama
- Public
- Suffrage
- Music
- Destiny
- Future
- Evolution
- Protection
- Education
- Clothes
- Nuclear
- Renaissance

- Herstory
- Blame
- Environment
- Domination
- Third World
- Asian
- Global
- Restrained
- Racism
- Storytelling
- Timeline
- Context
- Caucasian
- Voice
- Crusade
- Time
- Village
- Border
- Revolution
- Primordial
- I.Q.
- DNA
- Communism

- Ourstory
- Inquisition
- Power
- Democracy
- Self-actualization
- War
- Foreshadow
- Truth
- Women
- Power
- Library
- Homogeneous
- Brain
- Vote
- Territory
- Radical
- Fundamental
- Weapon
- Grow
- Control
- Neanderthal
- Cubicle
- Boredom

KID PIX® PLANNING SHEET

Title Slide

Buttons/Links: _____

Notes (Text/Sounds/Animations): _____

Slide 1

Buttons/Links: _____

Notes (Text/Sounds/Animations): _____

Slide 2

Buttons/Links: _____

Notes (Text/Sounds/Animations): _____

Slide 3

Buttons/Links: _____

Notes (Text/Sounds/Animations): _____

Slide 4

Buttons/Links: _____

Notes (Text/Sounds/Animations): _____

Slide 5

Buttons/Links: _____

Notes (Text/Sounds/Animations): _____

HYPERSTUDIO® PLANNING SHEET

Title Card

Buttons/Links: _____

Notes (Text/Sounds/Animations): _____

Card 1

Buttons/Links: _____

Notes (Text/Sounds/Animations): _____

Card 2

Buttons/Links: _____

Notes (Text/Sounds/Animations): _____

Card 3

Buttons/Links: _____

Notes (Text/Sounds/Animations): _____

Card 4

Buttons/Links: _____

Notes (Text/Sounds/Animations): _____

Card 5

Buttons/Links: _____

Notes (Text/Sounds/Animations): _____

CLARISWORKS® STORYBOARD PLANNING SHEET

Name: _____   Project: _____

Slide # _____

Words/Narration: _____

_____

_____

_____

_____

_____

Slide # _____

Words/Narration: _____

_____

_____

_____

_____

_____

Slide # _____

Words/Narration: _____

_____

_____

_____

_____

_____

Slide # _____

Words/Narration: _____

_____

_____

_____

_____

_____

SOFTWARE PUBLISHERS

Davidson and Associates

19840 Pioneer Ave.

Torrance, CA 90503

(800) 545-7677

Discis Knowledge Research, Inc.

P.O. Box 66

Buffalo, NY 14223-0066

(800) 567-4321

Edmark

P.O. Box 3218

Redmond, WA 98073-3218

(800) 426-0856

EduQuest/IBM

One Culver Road

Dayton, NJ 08810-9988

(800) 426-3327

Grolier Electronic Publishing

Sherman Turnpike

Danbury, CT 06816

(800) 356-5590

Lawrence Productions

1800 South 35th Street

Galesburg, MI 49053

(616) 665-7075

MECC

6160 Summit Drive North

Minneapolis, MN 55430-4003

(800) 685-6322

Microsoft Corproation

One Microsoft Way

Redmond, WA 98052

(800) 426-9400

National Geographic Educational Software

P.O. Box 98018

Washington, D.C. 20090-8018

(800) 368-2728

Scholastic, Inc.

2931 East McCarty Street

P.O. Box 7502

Jefferson City, MO 65102-9968

(800) 541-5513

Tom Snyder Productions

80 Coolidge Hill Road

Watertown, MA 02172

(800) 342-0236

Troll Associates

100 Corporate Drive

Mahwah, NJ 07498-0025

(800) 526-5289

REFERENCES AND RESOURCES

Social Studies Information

National Council for the Social Studies

The Instructional Technology Committee of National Council for the Social Studies has established a list server for interested Internet users to share information and ideas about social studies education in grades K–12 and in teacher education. To subscribe to the listservs and receive e-mail messages posted there, follow these steps:

- Send an e-mail message to: listproc2@bgu.edu

- Leaving the subject line blank, send the following message: SUBSCRIBE NCSS-L { your Internet address}.

- For example: "SUBSCRIBE NCSS-L teacher@school.edu".

Web sites

The following may be able to provide information to you.

- Center for Civic Education—*http://www.civiced.org/*

- National Geographic—*http://www.nationalgeographic.com*

- United States Department of Education—*http://www.ed.gov*

- American Educators Research Association—*http://aera.net*

- American Federation of Teachers—*http://www.aft.org*

- National Educators Association—*http://www.nea.org*

- National Institute for Literacy—*http://www.nifl.gov/*

- American Library Association—*http://www.ala.org*

- Center for Excellence in Education—*http://cee.indiana.edu*

REFERENCES AND RESOURCES *(cont.)*

Books

Dewey, John. *Education and Experience.* Collier Macmillan Publishers, 1938.

Kohn, Alfie. *Beyond Discipline.* ACSD, 1996.

Kohn, Alfie. *Punished by Rewards.* Houghton Mifflin Company, 1993.

Lazerson, Marvin and McLauglin, McPherson, & Bailey. *An Education of Value.* Cambridge University Press, 1987.

Loewen, James. *Lies My Teacher Told Me.* The New Press, 1995.

Ohanian, Susan. *Who's In Charge?* Boynton/Cook Publishers, 1994.

Postman, Neil. *The End of Education.* Alfred A. Knopf, 1995.

Teacher Created Materials—Social Studies

2206—Technology Connections for Westward Movement

2202—Technology Connections for the Civil War

2203—Technology Connections for Colonial America

2024—The Twenties

2025—The Thirties

2026—The Forties

2027—The Fifties

2028—The Sixties

2029—The Seventies

2100—The 20th Century

497—Focus on Presidents

2102—Ancient History Simulations

481—World History Simulations

480—American History Simulations

470—Our Fifty States

1157—Wonders of the World GeoSafari® Lesson Card Packs

664—Geography of the Continents

REFERENCES AND RESOURCES *(cont.)*

Catalogs

- **Social Studies School Service** is perhaps one of the most comprehensive sources of social studies materials. 10200 Jefferson Blvd, Culver City, CA 90232

- **Nystrom** announces a new, free catalog of maps, globes, atlases, and curriculum materials for social studies. Please contact Nystrom at 3333 Elston Avenue, Chicago, IL 60618, (800)621-8086 or visit our Web site, NystromNet, at http://www.nystromnet.com.

- **The National Center for Research on Cultural Diversity and Second Language Learning** has a catalog of research reports, educational practice reports, occasional papers, and videos of interest to educators with English language learners in their classrooms. Contact NCRCDSLL at 1118 22nd Street, NW, Washington, DC 20037, or 202-429-9292, or visit NCRCDSLL on line at http://www.cal.org/

- **The Campanian Society, Inc.** publishes an Educational Materials Catalog containing information about teaching packs, books, videos, games, and posters for teaching about the ancient world— Egypt, Greece, Rome and the Middle Ages and many materials on ancient mythology. Contact The Campanian Society, Inc., Box 167, Oxford, Ohio 45056; telephone (513) 524-4846; Fax (513) 524-0276; e-mail *campania@one.net*

- **Enslow Publishers, Inc.,** has released a spring 1996 catalog which features more than 300 K–12 nonfiction library books that explore a variety of subjects. Each series of books featured is categorized by reading level and is preceded by a brief summary. A description of each title is provided along with other relevant information, such as age level. For more information, contact Enslow Publishers, Inc., 44 Fadem Road, Box 699, Springfield, NJ 07081-0699; 800-398-2504 (toll free phone) or 201-379-7940 (fax).

- **Crystal Productions** produces an annual Social Studies Resources Catalog. The resources were specifically produced and selected for the studies of humanities, American and world history, geography, and multicultural studies in elementary, middle, and secondary schools and colleges. The materials include videos, videodiscs, CD-ROMs, time lines, poster prints, portfolio prints, multimedia kits, books, maps, and games. For more information, contact Crystal Productions, Box 2159, Glenview, IL 60025; 800-255-8629; 800-657-8149 (fax).

MISCELLANEOUS RESOURCES

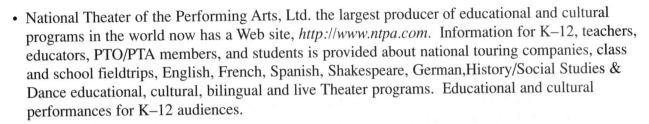

- National Theater of the Performing Arts, Ltd. the largest producer of educational and cultural programs in the world now has a Web site, *http://www.ntpa.com*. Information for K–12, teachers, educators, PTO/PTA members, and students is provided about national touring companies, class and school fieldtrips, English, French, Spanish, Shakespeare, German,History/Social Studies & Dance educational, cultural, bilingual and live Theater programs. Educational and cultural performances for K–12 audiences.

- NCSS member Alan Haskvitz has a new IBM disk available titled Hundreds of Free, Inexpensive, and Valuable Resources for Social Studies Teachers. The disk contains sections on the westward movement, global sources, economics, geography, history, political science, the environment, and general resources. The disk is written for 3.1 Windows. A booklet is also available. Haskvitz has received the NCSS Middle School Teacher of the Year Award, NCSS's first Exemplary Program Award, and the Christa McAuliffe Award. For more information, contact: Alan Haskvitz at 909-945-9942.

- O'Reilly & Associates has announced "WebSite for Teachers," a World Wide Web server for classroom use. Web Site allows Windows-using educators to create and "serve" electronic information and to make it available on an internal computer network for students only or on the Internet to any of the Web's estimated eight million users. Web Site is priced at $99 plus tax and shipping. For more information, contact:

    Mary Leal, O'Reilly & Associates, Inc. 103 Morris Street, Suite A,

    Sebastopol, CA 95472

    800-998-9938, ext. 254 (toll free), 707-829-0515, ext. 254 (phone), 707-829-9043 (fax), or mary@ora.com (e-mail).

- Scantron Quality Computers has announced the nationwide launch of the National Technology Coordinators Network (NTCN). NTCN is a support and research network dedicated to serving the needs of school technology coordinators. The network provides users with access to international e-mail, lesson plans, grant information, network and staff development issues, online discussion forums, and the purchasing power of a national consortium. For more information, contact:

    Scantron Quality Computers

    P.O. Box 349, St. Clair Shores, MI 48080

    800-777-3642 (toll free) or *ntcn@qualitycomp.com* (e-mail).

- Children's Television Workshop (CTW) has teamed up with telecommunications organizations such as AT&T and Pacific Bell to launch a literacy project connecting teachers and students in New York with teachers and students in California. The project, called Ghostwriter Classroom Connection, combines the power of CTW's multimedia show Ghostwriter with Integrated Service Data Network (ISDN) technology to promote literacy, especially among fourth and fifth grade

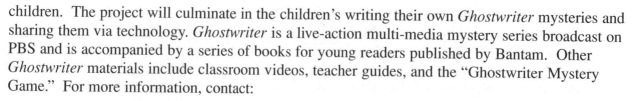

children. The project will culminate in the children's writing their own *Ghostwriter* mysteries and sharing them via technology. *Ghostwriter* is a live-action multi-media mystery series broadcast on PBS and is accompanied by a series of books for young readers published by Bantam. Other *Ghostwriter* materials include classroom videos, teacher guides, and the "Ghostwriter Mystery Game." For more information, contact:

Children's Television Workshop

One Lincoln Plaza, New York, NY 10023

212-595-3456.

• NCSS has expanded its information literacy packet to include the American Association of School Librarians (AASL) position statement "Information Literacy: A Position Paper on Information Problem Solving" that was endorsed by the NCSS Board of Directors in April. Copies of the complete packet, which includes NCSS Essential Social Studies Skills and two related ERIC Digests or the AASL statement are available from NCSS Information Services. To order, send a $0.32 self-addressed, stamped envelope to:

NCSS Information Services

ATTN: INFORMATION LITERACY

3501 Newark Street, NW, Washington, DC 20016.

• *"Simulations for Elementary and Primary School Social Studies,"* an annotated list of almost 200 simulations compiled by NCSS member Sharon Pray Muir, appears in the March 1996 issue of *Simulation & Gaming: An International Journal of Theory, Practice, and Research* (Volume 27, Number 1, pp. 41-73). The article updates a 1980 list that was published in Social Education. Single issues of S&G can be ordered for $16 from

Sage Publications

2455 Teller Road, Thousand Oaks, CA 91320

805-499-0721 (phone) or 805-499-0871 (fax).

• The National Center for Research on Cultural Diversity and Second Language Learning Has a video series, *Meeting the Challenge of Teaching Linguistically Diverse Students,* which presents some of the most effective instructional practices currently being used by teachers of linguistically and culturally diverse students. Classroom scenes illustrate each discussion. All videos have an accompanying training guide with theoretical and resource information and suggestions for using the videos in a wide variety of professional development formats. The videos include: VS1: Profile of Effective Bilingual Teaching Kindergarten VS2: Profile of Effective Bilingual Teaching: First Grade VS3: Instructional Conversations: Understanding Through Discussion VS4: Profile of Effective Teaching in a Multilingual Classroom VS5 Profile of Effective Two-Way Bilingual

MISCELLANEOUS RESOURCES *(cont.)*

Education: Sixth Grade, VS6: Learning Together: Two-Way Bilingual Immersion Programs. All videos are $40. Mail pre-payment (check or purchase order, payable to the Center for Applied Linguistics) to

Dissemination Coordinator, NCRCDSLL, Center for Applied Linguistics

1118 22nd Street, NW, Washington, DC 20037

Include a 10% shipping fee. For more information, call (202) 429-9292.

- Nystrom's family of award-winning atlases are a great resource and teaching tool for every classroom. Request a free catalog by contacting:

  Nystrom

  3333 Elston Avenue, Chicago, IL 60618

  (800) 621-8086

  Or visit our Web site, NystromNet, at http://www.nystromnet.com.

- Twenty-Five Lessons in Citizenship by D.L. Hennessey provides clear, concise, and accurate information about U.S. history and the make-up of national, county, and city governments for people who are studying to become citizens of the United States. It also contains question-and-answer sections, suggestions for teachers, and the entire text of the U.S. Constitution. Order online or by mail. For more info visit:

  http://members.aol.com/Bozokitty2/index.html

- *Celebrations Around the World: A Multicultural Handbook* by Carole S. Angell has just been published by Fulcrum Publishing of Golden, CO. Arranged by month, this book provides the teacher, librarian, clergy and others with a complete, up-to-date resource for world holidays, festivals and celebrations. Included are the background for each celebration as well as numerous activities. Ms. Angell is a Northern Virginia teacher/author who wrote this book primarily because she needed it for her multicultural classroom and could not find anything like it. The book is available from Fulcrum at (800) 992-2908.

- *Integrating Language and Culture in Middle School American History Classes* by D. Short describes a project that investigated the academic language of social studies and implemented instructional lessons designed to teach language and content skills to English language learners. ($4.00) Mail pre-payment (check or purchase order, payable to the Center for Applied Linguistics) to:

  Dissemination Coordinator, NCRCDSLL/Center for Applied Linguistics

  1118 22nd Street, NW, Washington, DC 20037

  Include a 10% shipping fee. For more information, call (202) 429-9292.

MISCELLANEOUS RESOURCES *(cont.)*

- *Attributes of Effective Programs and Classrooms Serving English Language Learners* by D. August and L. Pease-Alvarez, specifies the various conditions that maximize second language learners' opportunities to meet challenging outcome expectations. Their school change model is organized around two broad categories: school-wide culture, policies, and practice; and classroom culture, policies, and practice. Exemplars from schools across the U.S. provide concrete examples of effective practice. ($10.00) Mail pre-payment (check or purchase order, payable to the Center for Applied Linguistics) to: Dissemination Coordinator, NCRCDSLL/Center for Applied Linguistics

  1118 22nd Street, NW, Washington, DC 20037

  Include a 10% shipping fee. For more information, call 202-429-9292.

- *Ed.Net Briefs* is sent weekly to subscribers via e-mail throughout the academic school year from September to June. There is no charge for this service. To add your e-mail address to the subscriber list or to submit contributions for future Ed.Net Briefs newsletters, visit the Class IV Publications Web site at

  http://www.edbriefs.com/briefs.html and fill out the subscription form or the message box. The Web site also features an extensive list of linked online education resources.

- *Reach Every Child* lists over 2000 good resources for teachers and students. Everything from Web sites to minority organizations and locations to acquire quality primary resources is listed. It comes in both IBM or Macintosh format or as a book of about 200 pages. The best thing about this resource is that it was done by a teacher for teachers. It also has a large section of free materials. For more information write, Reach Every Child at 642 Chaparel, Mira Loma, CA 91762. The price is $22 with yearly updates available. Other sections include all Olympic organizations, agriculture sites, government contacts, Freedom of Information explanations and the best places to find both global, and United States social studies materials. All told there are 30 separate categories.

- *The Grant Network Review* is an excellent monthly publication featuring state, federal and foundation grants targeting K–12 educational programs. Publication is read by over one hundred schools throughout the country. Contact: Frank Turner, Fax: 213-293-4823 to request subscription information.

- The National Council for Accreditation of Teacher Education (NCATE) has announced the publication of its 41st annual guide, titled *Teacher Preparation: A Guide to Colleges and Universities*. The guide includes listings of professional development schools and nontraditional programs, along with lists of schools that have met specialized professional association guidelines. Specific information about the institutions includes degrees and programs, tuition, enrollment figures, faculty information, admission tests for initial preparation programs, nontraditional routes to licensure, scholarship information, and contact information. This year, for

the second time, the guide is being mailed to head counselors at the 3,000 largest high schools in the nation. To order the guide, send a check or purchase order for $15 to

NCATE

2010 Massachusetts Avenue, NW, Suite 500, Washington, DC 20036-1023,

Or call 202-466-7496 for a publications order form.

- Beacham Publishing has announced the publication of *The Look-It-Up Guide to Washington Libraries and Archives*. This resource serves as a comprehensive, up-to-date guide for locating Washington-area library and archival resources, including government, public, university, and special collections. The soft cover version costs $19; the library edition costs $39. For more information call 800-466-9644.

- Tarry Lindquist is the author of a new book titled *Seeing the Whole Through Social Studies*, published by Heinemann. The book is about reorganizing curriculum and choosing instructional strategies to make learning integrative, meaningful, value based, active, and challenging for both teachers and students. Lindquist has been recognized as NCSS Elementary Teacher of the Year and as a national Good Neighbor Award winner by State Farm. Currently a fifth-grade teacher at Lakeridge Elementary on Mercer Island, Washington, Lindquist also serves on the National Board for Professional Teaching Standards Middle Childhood/Generalist Committee. For more information, contact

Heinemann

361 Hanover Street, Portsmouth, NH 03801-3912

603-431-7894 (phone), 603-431-7840 (fax), or 603-431-4971 (fax).

- Eliminating Grades ASQC Quality Press has released a briefing titled *Eliminating Grades in School: An Allegory for Change*. Author Carol Sager offers alternatives to grades and discusses the pros and cons of different methods of achievement measurement. Special attention is given to the issue of whether or not using grades is an effective way to measure students' achievements, and how quality principles can be used to help resolve systematic problems and build consistency for change. This resource is 44 pages, softcover, and costs $12.00 plus $4.00 for shipping and processing. To order or receive more information, contact

ASQC Quality Press

611 East Wisconsin Avenue, Milwaukee, WI 53202,

800-248-1946.

NOTES